Glory, The Struggle For Yards

Inspiration from Turn of the Century African-American Unsung Heroes

GARY S. BURLEY,
RALPH V. BROOKS AND
DONNA T. FRANCAVILLA

GLORY, THE STRUGGLE FOR YARDS
INSPIRATION FROM TURN OF THE CENTURY
AFRICAN-AMERICAN UNSUNG HEROES

iUniverse books may be ordered through booksellers or by contacting:

iUniverse
1663 Liberty Drive
Bloomington, IN 47403
www.iuniverse.com
844-349-9409

ISBN: 978-1-6632-5395-8 (sc)
ISBN: 978-1-6632-5397-2 (hc)
ISBN: 978-1-6632-5396-5 (e)

Library of Congress Control Number: 2023911459

Print information available on the last page.

iUniverse rev. date: 01/22/2024

Contents

Dedication Page v

Acknowledgments vii

Thanking Others xiv

Introduction..xvii

Chapter 1   Breaking new ground as the First Minority
             Referee in any professional sport in North America
             succeeding despite being "Undefeated, Untied,
             Uninvited".. 1
Chapter 2   The First Paid African-American Black Football Player ...19
Chapter 3   First Haitian Black Professional American Football
             Player 29
Chapter 4   One of the First Black African-Americans to play
             College Football.. 37
Chapter 5   Fritz Pollard: First Black Coach in the National
             Football League 46

About the Authors

Who is Gary Burley? 87

Who is Co-Author Ralph Brooks?.. 111

Meet Co-Author, Editor, and Former CBS Journalist...................... 117

Meet Dr. Valencia Belle..128

Editor's Note 131

Dedication Page

This book is dedicated to my wife, **Bobbie Knight Burley**. She was elected as the fifteenth president, and First African-American Female to hold that honor at Miles College in Birmingham.

I was able to play in the NFL league for ten years amongst other great veterans. I chased quarterbacks all over the field but learned that running in a straight line is the fastest way to the quarterback.

What can I say, to the love of my life, my best friend and favorite first lady who has been by my side through cancer recovery and never allowed me to let go of my faith in God and his unchanging hands.

She is my rock through difficult surgeries and ongoing health issues. While taking care of me, she still found a way for 37 years to keep the lights on for the people in Birmingham, Alabama before retiring in 2016 as Vice President of Alabama Power Company.

This book is a gift of gratitude, respect, admiration, and praise for my wife, who means the world to me.

Gary (left) & Bobbie (right)

Acknowledgments

The authors would like to thank many people who contributed time, insight, expertise, and assistance.

Dave Smith, played wide receiver for three NFL teams: the Pittsburgh Steelers from 1970 to 1972, the Houston Oilers in 1972, and the Kansas City Chiefs in 1973. Courtesy of Indiana University of Pennsylvania, IUP Special Collections and University Archives, provided by Dr. Harrison Wick, Associate Professor at IUP Library

In 2014, **Pittsburgh Steelers tight end David Smith** called Gary Burley with the book-writing idea. He envisioned creating an exhibit that showcased the unknown original African-American football players and demonstrated their fortitude.

Unfortunately, David became ill and died before his dream was realized. His legacy is being carried out by Gary Burley and his team who have worked to assemble the information contained in these pages. The authors feel everyone can be inspired by these early, brave pioneers in football.

Dave Lewis Smith is an Indiana University of Pennsylvania (IUP) Athletic Hall of Fame member and a former professional American football player who was born in New York City, New York on May 18, 1947, and died on May 16, 2020, at the age of 73.

He played college football and basketball at Waynesburg University, a private college in Pennsylvania, and at IUP, Indiana University of Pennsylvania.

Hard-working Smith was remembered for his athleticism, hard work, and dedication. He was so determined not to miss a game, that he flew directly from catching a 62-yard touchdown pass in the 1968 Boardwalk Bowl in Atlantic City to a college basketball game at then-rival Geneva that same night.

Smith played offense and defense for the IUP football team.

Known for wearing a number 88 jersey, Smith was inducted into the **IUP Athletic Hall of Fame** in 1997.

Jack Bennett, the voice of the Crimson Hawks, told *WCCS-FM 101.1* that Dave Smith was one of the greatest athletes he had ever seen.

"In addition to being a football and basketball player, he was an outstanding player in baseball too. He probably set the tone for later years of players who were drafted by the NFL teams then went on either as a player or a coach in the NFL because he was the first after his senior year at IUP."

The first African player to be drafted

Dave Smith became the first African-American player drafted from IUP by a National Football League team.

He played wide receiver for three NFL teams: the **Pittsburgh Steelers** from (1970 to 1972), the **Houston Oilers** (1972), and the **Kansas City Chiefs** (1973). According to the **Pro Football Hall of Fame**, Smith, a member of the IUP Hall of Fame, died May 16, 2020, in Washington, D.C.

DAVE SMITH

Dave Smith in 1969
Dave Smith played wide receiver for three NFL teams: the Pittsburgh
Steelers from 1970 to 1972, the Houston Oilers in 1972, and the
Kansas City Chiefs in 1973. Courtesy of Indiana University of
Pennsylvania, IUP Special Collections and University Archives, provided
by Dr. Harrison Wick, Associate Professor at IUP Library

Gary Burley remembers the phone call with Dave Smith when he shared his vision for a book and exhibit. It was the last time Gary spoke to him. Dave envisioned that the little-known athletes who broke the color barrier around the turn of the century be written about.

The authors honor his memory by making Dave Smith's dreams finally come true.

FOOTBALL

ROW 1 J. Clark, J. Heimlich, G. Pawlowski, D. Buzzelli, G. Stair, H. Harvey, B. Tate. ROW 2 G. Persechetti, M. Priest, C. Ruffner, W. Blucas, D. Draganac, B. Frederick, D. Smith. ROW 3 B. Dobies, S. Moley, S. Rosso, J. Steppling, S. Patti, H. Kaufman, J. Kovalchick. ROW 4 J. Voit, G. Stark, J. Neptune, C. Costazzo, T. Pipkins, D. Weber, A. Brill. ROW 5 B. Lasser, T. Oleson, J. Paul, B. Barto, M. Finnerty, D. Corey, B. Rapsk, J. Kantner. ROW 6 C. Klausing, head coach; T. Kerin, student trainer; J. Patalsky, student trainer; B. Cochran, student trainer; J. Bean, manager; T. Getner, manager.

1969 Oak Yearbook - Football Team
Dave Smith: Last player on the right, 2nd row
Courtesy of Indiana University of Pennsylvania, IUP
Special Collections and University Archives provided by Dr.
Harrison, Wick, Associate Professor at IUP Library

Gary Burley (left) and Charles Barkley (right)
in Birmingham, Alabama

A special thank-you goes to television analyst and former professional basketball player **Charles Barkley,** who, in his frank and authentic style encourages us to live an unconventional life, live in the moment, and understand that life only exists while you are alive.

"People who are successful in life live in the present moment and not the future but the most important thing is to learn from the past lessons."

Gary Burley's agent Co-founder of the Fritz Pollard Alliance John B. Wooten

We appreciate the insights and contributions of former American football guard and agent **John B. Wooten**, who played nine professional seasons in the NFL for the Cleveland Browns and Washington Redskins.

Wooten played college football at the **University of Colorado** and was drafted in the fifth round of the 1959 NFL Draft. He was named to the **College Football Hall of Fame** in 2012 and is a member of CU's All-Century Team, the Browns' Ring of Honor, and the Browns' Legends Club.

After retiring from football, Wooten worked for a short time as a sports agent. His company was called *Pro Sports Advisors.* The company operated from 1973 to 1975 when he represented Gary Burley.

He thought back to the days he represented Burley. "Burley was in the league from '75-'84. Gary was the last group that I represented as an agent."

"Gary has been a great soldier for us," he told co-author Donna Francavilla during a 2022 Zoom phone call. "The things I remember about Gary Burley is that he was a real good football player and we saw that from his work ethic and how he went about his business and was the kind of person we wanted to represent us in the NFL. Gary was trained not only as a player but also knowing what it takes to be successful as a player in the NFL."

During the interview, Wooten fondly remembered evaluating Gary. "We felt he could play at this level so that's how we ended up recruiting him."

"The thing about Gary that I felt so strongly about was we knew that he was a good football player but he was so committed to the community and all that he's around and you still see that one-on-one caring today. That's the thing you really look for as it relates to players. Good character makes you do things that aren't easy to do. Get up, work out, work out on your own, and be a part of the community that you're involved in, but work in the community to make it a better place. You see the golf tournaments that he puts on. In the old days, we had Black players who lived in the cities because of segregation, which wasn't a bad thing because players worked hard to improve their community."

The authors collectively hope to continue the mission of improving the lives of young people by writing this book. They seek to preserve the stories of former great football players and to collect comments and observations from journalists who documented those achievements.

After leaving the Bengals, Wooten then became a scout with the Dallas Cowboys from 1975 to 1979. He was promoted to Director of Pro Personnel in 1980. In 1992, he moved to the role of Player Personnel with the Philadelphia Eagles. He was promoted to Vice President of Player Personnel in 1994. In 1998, he moved to the Baltimore Ravens as Assistant Director of Pro and College Scouting. In 2000, he began to prepare for his eventual retirement, taking a step back to work as a consultant with the Ravens until 2003. In 2003, Wooten became the Chairman of the Fritz Pollard Alliance which is an advocacy group that works in conjunction with the NFL as it relates to minority hiring in coaching, scouting, and front office positions.

"From 1933-1946 there were no Black players in the league because White owners took the position that the Black players were taking the jobs away from White players. So they just cut it out. And then when they came back and they wanted Paul Brown to bring his club to Cleveland, that's when a lot of this stuff changed."

Wooten took the time to speak with us about the remarkable contributions some of these players made to the ever-evolving sport. Thank you for your support!

Bootsy Collins (left) and Gary Burley (right) at Gary's & Bobbie's house in Birmingham, Alabama after the entertainer was the grand marshal of the Magic City Classic parade in 2013

We'd also like to thank the all-time great funk and R&B bassist, singer, bandleader, and music producer:

~

Bootsy Collins

Bootsy Collins had this to say about the book:

"This amazing book is all about unknown stories of the African-American Pioneers that have paved the way for both past & present NFL Players. **In this book, you will have the chance to experience the game without putting on a helmet or shoulder pads.** I have been a big fan of football since playing as a kid, but after being hit & broken up a few times, I realized I need to play music instead. Lol! Football is a reflection of Hard Knocks Life. My friend, Gary Burley, not only talked the talk, but he also walked the walk. You can read all about football's beginnings right here, right now."

–Bootsy Baby

Thanking Others

We are humbled by the endorsements and comments from Jim Foster who hosts *YouTube's* The *Bengal Jim's Tailgate,* "The stories in this book are amazing! So glad they are being told."

We'd like to thank artist Tony Jannetto and book cover designer Leon Moody for their creativity.

We'd also like to acknowledge the many media outlets, journalists, broadcasters, stations, newspapers and magazines including but not limited to *The Shelia Smoot Radio Show on WAGG and CBS-42 and Focus with Shelia Smoot and Ronda Robinson on ABC 33/40 and Birmingham's CBS-42's Sherry Jackson* for hosting us. Thank you to Birmingham's *Talk 99's Jeffery Rush* on the *Your Security Guys Radio Show,* WUTG-FM Tuscaloosa Talk Show Host of *Inside The Juke Joint & Musician Lenard Brown, The Rick and Bubba Show, Alabama Media Professionals, Alabama News Center's* Mark Kelly, *B-Metro's* publisher Joe O'Donnell, thank you for believing in us and helping us with a book that could change people's lives.

We want to give a shout-out to Darlene A. and Mac Greco, *Sawyer Solutions LLC,* and author, movie producer, and speaker *Edie Hand* for their support.

We are so appreciative of the unending support from *Hudson Group* Vice President of Operations in charge of retail stores in airports across Al, MS, GA, and LA Carol McElheney. Without your help, we could not have let readers know about the incredible accomplishments and sacrifices made by pre and early NFL Players. Thanks for giving us a platform for spreading the word.

We'd also like to express our thanks to *Humana Medicare Advantage* for recognizing the importance of diversity and inclusion. Shout out to

Mark Riddlesworth, Alyssa Reynolds, Vicki Perryman, JoAnn Garcia, Billy Bonaparte, Ed Offner, Lanita Harris-Bibbs, Orinthous Richardson, John Barger, Khursheed Zafar, Dwayne McCalla, Ayana Bailey, Sandra Marshall, Jamie White, and Webster Rose. Ralph Brooks said, "I just wanted to let you all know how much I appreciate the positive impact you had on my life at Humana, the place where I have worked for 17 years. I am eternally grateful. We will always be family."

Thank you to attorney Ken Guin and business consultant Bill J.W. Thomas for legal and business consulting help. Thank you to Frankly Speaking Communications LLC for the content development, research, promotional, marketing and publicity provided. Without the considerable input of the company's talents and skills, this book wouldn't be as thoroughly researched, easy to read and widely distributed. Thanks for your help in telling our stories and the stories of these 5 outstanding individuals. Thank you also to Dianca Woods and Isis M. Jones LLC for assistance with spreading the word.

Resource libraries include **Geneva Historical Society**, in Geneva, New York, the **University of San Francisco Special Collections & University Archives in San Francisco**, California, Dr. Harrison Wick, Associate Professor, **Special Collections Librarian and University Archive, Indiana University of Pennsylvania (IUP Libraries).** Thank you for granting us permission to reprint your precious photographs and thank you for your contributions **John Hay Library** at the **University Library** in Providence, Rhode Island, and home to **Brown University**, remarkable collections of rare books. And many thanks to Bryce Horton, **Hoover Public Library**, Alabama, for an author's interview, hosting us, and importantly, conducting extensive research on our behalf.

We'd like to say a special thank you to Quintard Taylor, founder of BlackPast.org.

We'd like to give a special thank you to the **University of San Francisco Special Collections & University Archives** for the use of the rare college photos of Burl Toler.

Thank you to YouTube's **Bengal Jim's Tailgate Experience** and to YouTube's **Larry Smith,** Evening News Anchor at WLEX-TV for the pre-publishing interviews.

Thank you to Scott Myers at the **Alabama Sports Hall of Fame**. Many thanks for all you've done.

We appreciate your patience and trust in us. We could not have done this project without all of you.

Introduction

Glory - The Struggle for Yards is a book about some of the nearly forgotten first Black NFL players who broke the color barrier around the turn of the century.

These remarkable men, Hall of Famer **Burl Toler**, the Black Cyclone **Charles Follis,** Motorcycle McDonald **Henry McDonald**, the Warrior of his Time **Gideon Smith**, and the Human Torpedo **Fritz Pollard** played the sport with dedication despite experiencing segregation, racism, trials, and tribulations. This book explores the many firsts they accomplished despite enduring an uphill battle.

They had to prove themselves as players of equal strength, ability, and talent as their non-colored counterparts.

Little had been known about some of these players but exhaustive research revealed tales of courage, determination, and true grit.

Be prepared to be inspired by their suppressed *Glory,* inspired by their struggle and their *Struggle for Yards*.

Burl Toler #85 Linebacker
in university GreenScrapbookpl in 1950
Photo Credit: University of San Francisco Special Collections Archives, San
Francisco, CA

Chapter 1

Breaking new ground as the First Minority Referee in any professional sport in North America succeeding despite being "Undefeated, Untied, Uninvited"

Legendary veteran NFL commissioner Pete Rozelle thought so much of this humble African-American athlete, the 30-year veteran made a gutsy, pivotal decision.

In 1965, the same year President Lyndon Johnson signed the Voting Rights Act into law, Peter Rozelle chose to elevate a Black man to the official role.

The athlete who wore jersey number 37 for most of his career traded it in for a referee's uniform. This sports aficionado transitioned from actively playing to carefully observing. And he stuck with it. He served as an official in the NFL for a quarter of a century.

Burl Abron Toler Sr. who suffered racial discrimination, is considered the **best** player on one of college football's greatest teams. Toler's team was denied a bowl bid despite a 9-0 record because it refused to leave its two Black players - Burl Toler and Ollie Matson - behind.

Burl A. Toler was also the first African-American to serve as a field official in a major American professional sports league. Known for his humility, strength of character, and credibility, this exemplary role model was appointed by the NFL as a head linesman.

Burl A. Toler transitioned into the role after his football playing career ended prematurely due to injury. Despite not being able to play, Toler made a lasting impact on the game when in the mid-1960s, he became the **first Black NFL official** and the **first Black Official in Super Bowl History.**

Toler officiated important games, including Super Bowl XIV in 1980, in which the Pittsburgh Steelers defeated the Los Angeles Rams.

Toler also officiated in the 1982 A.F.C. championship game, a game the Bengals' *Glory* co-author Gary Burley participated in.

The **Cincinnati Bengals** prevailed against the **San Diego Chargers** in a game known as **The Freezer Bowl.**

Gary recalls that the game was memorable because of its frigid temperatures, the coldest temperatures of any game in league history.

Gary Burley reflected: "I remember The Freezer Bowl game. We prayed before the game like we always did. The first guy I saw on the field was **Burl Toler** dressed in a referee's black and white striped shirt and solid black pants. Despite the cold, the referees didn't wear coats or scarves, or gloves. Toler's fingers became so cold, that he suffered from frostbite. It was 59 degrees below zero that day."

"Incredibly, I also spotted guys with their shirts off spelling out the name 'Bengals' each one with a letter painted on their chest. We played in subzero weather so cold you could spit, and before it hit the ground it was a ball of ice. We knew it was cold when shortly before the game began, we spotted vehicles driving across the Ohio River which separates Ohio and Kentucky. At the end of the memorable game, the announcer said, 'The Bengals are headed to the Super Bowl', which were words that thawed our frozen bodies!"

The wind chill in Cincinnati on Jan. 10, 1982, reached a frigid minus 59 degrees Fahrenheit. As Gary accurately recalled, records show Toler sustained frostbite on his fingers.

Facing Adversity

Burl faced adversity while still a young man. Burl's father, Arnold, worked as a modest Pullman porter. His mother, Annie King Toler, an educator, operated a small store and ran a boarding house. Young Burl was one of four children. Throughout his childhood, his parents stressed education. Burl went to a segregated high school. At the time, he did not play football because of a burn on his arm which happened when he disposed of a vat of cooking grease.

Upon graduating from high school, Toler decided to enroll at Lemoyne College in Memphis, Tennessee. Burl Toler's daughter, Susan Toler-Carr, told *NBC Sports* that her father left the racially-charged Memphis, Tennessee area for California to pursue a better life.

Burl Toler #55 (left) and Ollie Matson #33
at the end (right) in university GreenScrapbookpl in 1950
Photo Credit: University of San Francisco Special
Collections Archives, San Francisco, CA

Bruce Weber of *The New York Times* writes that after graduating, "Burl went to San Francisco at the suggestion of an uncle who lived there, and he enrolled at the two-year City College of San Francisco, where the football coach spotted him in the gymnasium and asked him to come out for the team."

In his first practice, the story goes, he tackled the star running back Ollie Matson on three consecutive plays. Susan Toler Carr remembered that her father told her he didn't know anything about football then.

"The coach saw him and recruited him to play."

After Burl tackled Ollie several times, "like Dominos" Susan said, "They got to know each other, and they became best friends from that."

Their 1948 team had a stellar 12-0 record earning both Toler and Matson scholarships at the University of San Francisco. Toler and Matson led their team to the **1948 Mythical Junior College National Championship**. Toler, who was perhaps the best player on one of college football's greatest teams together with Matson became the focus of racial discrimination.

Burl Toler #55 Linebacker in university GreenScrapbookpl diving for the football at practice in 1950 Photo Credit: University of San Francisco Special Collections Archives, San Francisco, CA

A *New York Times* article, reflecting on Burl Toler's life, writes, "The story of Toler's college team, the **1951 University of San Francisco Dons**, is one of the most extraordinary in sports." It appears the Dons were destined for a bowl game. It would have provided the school with badly-need funds to keep the football program alive.

After capping a 9-0 regular season with a 20-2 victory over Loyola at the **Rose Bowl**, USF received only a conditional invitation to the **Orange Bowl**.

It was not selected for a postseason game by the Southern-based bowl game committees.

We told them to 'Go to *Hell*'

According to a former team member, the late Bob St. Claire, the players would be invited to play in a bowl only if the team agreed the two

Black players wouldn't participate. It turned out to be a deal-breaker for the rest of their teammates.

St. Claire, a former USF defensive tackle and offensive end, told *CBS* in *Undefeated and Uninvited:*

"We were *all angry* that they would even *suggest* doing that, **leaving our two Black players behind.** These were teammates; these were *brothers.* The reason the league officially gave was because of the Don's weak schedule, but in truth, that excuse was given because the league didn't want to include its two Black players, Toler and Matson."

The Don's team collectively refused to sacrifice its two players even though money was needed to keep the football program going.

In a 2007 *Undefeated and Uninvited CBS* interview, a white-haired Burl Toler sat contemplatively on bleachers when he talked about what happened back in 1951. The 79-year-old echoed the team's resolve when he emphasized that the team acted in unison:

"That's the relationship we had with one another," he said as if he couldn't imagine it would work any other way. "If one can't go, don't ask for anyone else. We are a team and we're going to stay like that and do things as we've always done them."

Susan Toler-Carr told *CBS* that the team chose to stick together: On the YouTube recording, these guys said, '**No!** If Burl and Ollie can't go to the game, *we're not going to go.* That was the end of the football season. **They chose compassion** and what was right over money and fame. What I see is brotherly love. You can't tell there wasn't an earnest amount of **love and admiration.**"

At a 2011 event to commemorate the 60th anniversary of the team, St. Clair again recalled with pride, "**We told them to go to hell.**" That was the end of the football season because the team was not going without Ollie and Burl.

Sports Illustrated called the Dons "**the best team you never heard of.**" *The Times* observed that "The Dons sent nine players to the N.F.L., three of whom, —Gino Marchetti, Bob St. Clair, and Ollie Matson, —were eventually inducted into the **Professional Football Hall of Fame.**"

Head Coach Joe Kuharish went on to coach at Notre Dame and for three professional teams.

*Burl Toler (left) with Ollie Matson (right) at their Graduation celebration in 1952.
Photo Credit: University of San Francisco Special
Collections Archives, San Francisco, CA*

Pete Rozelle, who served as the athletic publicity director, later became the NFL commissioner. Ollie Matson was an American Olympic medal winning sprinter. Toler who played on the line on offense and linebacker on defense, was drafted by Cleveland, but he never made it to the pros because of a devastating knee injury in a college all-star game.

"I personally felt Burl Toler was the *best player of any of us,*" Gino Marchetti said. "He was the best tackler, the hardest hitter, and he had the most speed."

Burl Toler worked hard and played hard. He was a dedicated father of six, a husband, and an educator. Susan Toler-Carr recalled that her father worked five days a week at Benjamin Franklin Middle School in San Francisco as a teacher and as the district's first African-American secondary school principal. "And every Saturday morning, my mom would drive him to the airport, and on Sunday nights or Monday nights, she'd pick him up."

Toler inspired his family's next two generations to play the sport. Toler's son, Burl Jr., and his grandson, Burl III, played college football for the California Golden Bears.

Burl Toler #55 at his team practice in 1950.
Photo Credit: University of San Francisco Special
Collections Archives, San Francisco, CA

Facing Discrimination

Publicly and incredibly, Toler faced discrimination as a football player and as an official. The star linebacker on the Dons' famous **Undefeated, Untied, Uninvited** 1951 football team was **visibly shunned because of his skin color.**

Privately, Toler was said to have kept the *verbal and physical assaults* to himself, hiding the abuse from his children and colleagues. Jim Tunney worked on the same crew with Toler for 11 years. "Toler was so self-possessed," he told the *New York Times* after Toler's death, "that whatever racist attitudes he encountered in the game simply never became an issue. *He just didn't allow racism to enter into his doing his job,*" Tunney said. "He never mentioned it, and if it ever did occur, he just *rose above it.*"

It was Burl Toler's humility, character, and professionalism that caught Pete Rozelle's attention. The commissioner was so impressed by Toler, that he named him the *first African-American official in the league*. To fully appreciate this momentous move, it's important to put the decision in perspective.

Dating back to September of 1920 when the league was established, no Blacks had served in the NFL. Burl Toler was able to break a color barrier that had been in existence for more than 4 decades!

This move was symbolic as well as significant as it happened in the same year President Lyndon Johnson signed the voting rights act into law. The voting rights law contained information similar to the 15th

Amendment which protects the voting rights of all citizens regardless of race or the color of their skin.

Interestingly, Burl broke through the color barrier *after* being denied an opportunity to play in the Rose Bowl. He broke through the color barrier *after* being drafted by the Cleveland Browns as their 9th-round draft pick and number 105 overall. He broke through the color barrier *after* suffering a career-ending injury.

Burl didn't allow racial discrimination, prevalent at the time, to stop him from paving the way for African-American officials. Said his son Burt Toler Jr., "*He was a target, no doubt about it.*"

Burl Toler Jr. told *NBC Sports, Black History Month,* "His response always was: 'If he goes out and referees a good game and is fair in his responses, even though he's Black as long as he does a job well, he won't be the last.'

"He may have been the first but as long as he does his job well, he won't be the last African-American out there.'"

1950 Burl Toler, 2nd player (left) #85 on the front line in Team Photo
*Photo Credit: University of San Francisco Special Collections
& University Archives, San Francisco, CA*

His grandson, Burt Tamayo Toler III, a former Arena wide receiver, knew his grandfather was a pioneer: "I knew he was a trailblazer. I knew that he was special. He didn't go with the intention of being the first Black ref. In retrospect, it's an *amazing accomplishment* but it's even more amazing to me to know that he wanted to play football; his career got cut short, and then he still wanted to be around the game. Being a ref was the path that he was going to take and he was going to do anything he could in his ability to do that (referee)."

His children remember that Burl's only goal was to referee a good game. But his path wasn't an easy one.

Racially-Motivated Onslaughts

To physically protect himself when working as a referee, Burl Toler was reported to have worn a plastic protector under his hat. This shielded his eyes from the items irate fans threw at him. It's not something he spoke openly about. The protective shield was invisible from afar but noticed by his children. His son Martel Toler recalled that his father wore what looked to him like a plastic shell under his cap. When Martel asked his father about the shield, the elder Burl simply stated he wore the protective layer to protect his face *"because there are times when people throw stuff at me."*

Super Bowl Linesman

Burl Abron Toler Sr. was an African-American **pioneer** who went on to become the head linesman in Pittsburgh's 31-19 Super Bowl victory over the then-Los Angeles Rams in 1980.

A Principled Principal

Toler graduated from the University of San Francisco (USF) with a bachelor's degree in 1952 and then earned a master's degree in 1966. He was the **first Black secondary school principal at Ben Franklin Middle School in San Francisco.**

*1950 Burl Toler, 6ᵗʰ player #85 (left) on the front line and Ollie Matson #33,
3ʳᵈ player (left) in the backfield on Offensive Team.
Photo Credit: University of San Francisco Special Collections Archives,
San Francisco, CA*

Burl Toler's Legacy

Burl never strayed far from the game. He remained involved in the NFL as a Game Observer. What were his responsibilities? He graded officials. Burl served for eight years in this position. Burl Toler Sr. bravely broke the color barrier creating a continuing legacy that is remembered by the African-Americans who suit up in black and white uniforms.

He paved the way for Black officiating crew members such as Greg Steed, Julian Mapp, Dale Shaw, Jerome Boger, Barry Anderson, Carl Johnson, and Anthony Jeffries.

The father of six is credited with opening doors for men and women alike, including women of color such as Jennifer King, the first Black female assistant running back coach for the Washington Football Team, and Maia Chaka, a native of Rochester, New York who became the third female on-field official after Sarah Thomas and Shannon Eastiner.

Burt Toler is credited with inspiring generations that came after him with the knowledge that they too can achieve great things.

An idea whose time has come

According to *The Christian Science Monitor,* back in 1965, Pete Rozelle made it clear that he thought the climate was right and this was an idea whose time had come. Rozelle said he was hoping for some owners to *"make his day,"* as he put it, by taking these steps toward integration. As to why pro football has lagged behind major league baseball and pro basketball in hiring Black head coaches, the Commissioner said, he *"thought the problem was an old boys network."*

Rozelle never lost sight of the NFL one day evolving to having the first Black head football coach. Although Rozelle retired as commissioner in 1989, that same year, **Art Shell**, a two-time Super Bowl Champion, was named the *first NFL African-American head coach for the Oakland Raiders.* Gary Burley remembers Art Shell as a man of integrity. Burley recalled, "He holds the distinction of becoming the 2nd African-American head coach in the history of professional football. And the first in the sport's modern era. I remember facing off on the field against him."

In 2009, Bruce Weber of the *New York Times* explained the significance of Toler's talent and contributions to the sport:

"When Toler began his career, there were six on-field officials: the referee, who lines up behind the offensive backfield; the umpire, who is positioned in the middle of the field behind the defensive line; the head lineman and the line judge, who are on opposite sidelines on the line of scrimmage; the field judge, who stands on the sideline in the defensive backfield, and the back judge, who is positioned in midfield behind the defensive backs. A seventh official, the side judge, an across-the-field complement to the field judge, was added in 1978.

Weber goes on to observe, "For most of his career, Toler was a head linesman, with a twofold responsibility: first to watch for line-of-scrimmage infractions like being offside, and then to move downfield to monitor receivers running short and midrange pass routes and the defenders covering them."

Weber correctly noted that the "job requires not just the instinct to read plays as they develop and foot speed, but also because he lines up on the sideline and within easy shouting distance of coaches, an especially serene demeanor. Toler had to maintain the progression of the game. Nothing could distract him. He's looking at coaches, he's watching players coming in and out of the game, but mostly he's focused on the line-of-scrimmage infractions monitoring receivers and defenders covering them."

1951-Undefeated -University of San Francisco Dons, 2nd Row, (left) fifth in the row, Burl Toler #55, and on the same row seventh, Ollie Matson #33.

In all, Toler worked for 17 years at Benjamin Franklin Middle School in San Francisco as a teacher and secondary school principal. Toler also served on the Board of Trustees of his Alma Mater, the University of San Francisco from 1987 until 1998. He left a legacy – he had six children with his wife Melvia, and eight grandchildren and two brothers and one sister.

Toler along with Hall of Fame and Olympian Ollie Matson was initiated into the Kappa Alpha Psi fraternity in 1950. He died in Castro Valley, California on August 16, 2009, leaving a great legacy.

His grandson, Burl Toler III, carried on his grandfather's love for football. Burl Toler III was in his second stint and 9th season of coaching the football staff at his alma mater in 2023, as well as his sixth working with the wide receivers. He is also in his second campaign as the team's recruiting coordinator.

Burl Toler #85 Linebacker in university GreenScrapbookpl in 1950
Photo Credit: University of San Francisco Special Collections Archives, San
Francisco, CA

1950 Burl Toler, 6ᵗʰ player (left) to right
#55 on the front line in Team Photo
Photo Credit: University of San Francisco
Special Collections & University Archives,
San Francisco, CA

*Burl Toler #55 Linebacker in university
GreenScrapbookpl diving for the football
at practice in 1950
Photo Credit: University of San Francisco
Special Collections Archives, San
Francisco, CA*

*January 3, 1982: Cincinnati Bengals defensive lineman
Gary Burley celebrates with the crowd as the Bengals leave the field
after the AFC playoff win over the Buffalo Bills in Cincinnati.
The Bengals defensive unit shut down the Bulls in the
late minutes of the game to preserve the
Bengals' first playoff victory. AP PHOTO*

GARY'S INSIGHTS:

"In the 1982 Freezer Bowl, the first person I saw on the field was referee Burl Toler, the first African-American Ref. I didn't know history had unfolded in front of me when Burl became the first African-American to officiate the AFC/NFC championship game ever. Little did I know at the time that he was the first and withstood many trials and tribulations by being the First Black Man in that position. The anger and torment that he went through paved the way for others who followed his example. Today's players and referees benefit from his efforts."

Chapter One Timeline

Burl Abron Toler Sr.

- **Born:** May 09, 1928, Memphis, TN
- **Died:** August 16, 2009
- **Position:** American football official
- **Sports:** Football
- **Height:** 6 feet 2 in (1.87 m)
- **High School:** Memphis, TN (Manassas HS)
- **College:** LeMoyne (now LeMoyne-Owen), City College (CCSF) of San Francisco, and at the University of San Francisco
- **Professional:** Cleveland Browns and Chicago Cardinals
- **Career Awards:** NFL's First Black Official and Bay Area Sports Hall of Fame
- **Parents:** Annie King Toler and Arnold W. Toler, Sr.
- **Married to Melvia Woolfolk:** They had six children, three daughters, and three sons, and were also the proud grandparents of eight grandchildren. Toler's love for football was passed down to his son and grandson. Burl Toler, Jr., played college football for UC Berkeley, and Burl Toler, Jr.'s son, Burl Toler III, played in the NFL.

Accomplishments and Timeline

1948: While at City College of San Francisco, Toler teamed with future Dons teammate and NFL Hall-of-Famer Ollie Matson to lead the CCSF team to a 12-0 record and win the "Mythical" Junior College National Championship.

1950: Burl Toler along with " Hall of Famer" and Olympian Ollie Matson was initiated into the Kappa Alpha Psi fraternity (Gamma Alpha chapter) on April 17, 1950.

1951: Toler played for the legendary Don's football team after transferring to the University of San Francisco. The San Francisco Chronicle described the Dons as "one of the greatest colleges of all time." The book ***Undefeated, Untied and Uninvited***, the story of the 1951 University of San Francisco Dons has been turned into a screenplay by former San Francisco 49er player Jamie Williams.

1952: Toler earned his degree in science from USF and added a Master's in 1966. In the same year, Toler was drafted into the National Football League (NFL) by the Cleveland Browns. He injured his knee during a College All-Star game against the Los Angeles Rams, which ended his opportunity to play professional football. Shortly thereafter, he became a teacher at Benjamin Franklin Middle School in San Francisco. He also began officiating college games in the San Francisco area.

During the course of his 17-year career at Benjamin Franklin Middle School, Toler served as the *first African-American secondary school principal in the district.* The city council honored Toler by renaming the school Burl A. Toler Middle School. Toler was inducted into the City College and University of San Francisco Hall of Fame. He received several awards including the Isaac Hayes Achievement in Sports Award and the University of San Francisco Alumnus of the Year. The Burl A. Toler, Sr. Scholarship has been named in Toler's honor at St. Ignatius College Preparatory School in San Francisco.

1953: Burl Toler married his wife, Melvia Woolfolk.

1965: Burl became an NFL official with the help of NFL commissioner Pete Rozelle. Toler officiated for 25 years, from 1965-1989.

1980: Toler officiated in Super Bowl XIV in 1980, and wore the uniform number 37 for most of his career, except for the 1979–81 period, when officials were numbered by position.

1978: Toler served as San Francisco Police Department Commissioner from 1978 to 1986.

1987: He also served on the Board of Trustees at the University of San Francisco from 1987 to 1998.

1990: After retiring as an NFL official in 1990, for eight years he served as a game observer for the league, which involved grading officials.

2006: Honored as a *"Legend of the Hilltop"* as one of the top 75 athletes in USF history at the institution's 150th anniversary. In addition, The former Ben Franklin Middle School campus, now the home of two charter schools (Gateway High School and KIPP SF Bay Academy), was renamed in his honor on October 22, 2006.

2008: Toler became the third member of the 1951 Dons Football team inducted into the Bay Area Sports Hall of Fame in 2008, joining Matson and NFL Hall-of-Famers Gino Marchetti and Bob St. Clair.

2009: Burl Toler died at 81, the first African-American official in NFL history. Toler is survived by his brother Arnold of Memphis and six children - Valerie, Burl Jr., Susan, Gregory, Martel, and Jennifer and eight grandchildren.

2017: As a testament to Toler's excellence as a community leader, the University of San Francisco renamed Phelan Hall to become Toler Hall in May of 2017. According to a USF-sponsored article, Burl A. Toler was chosen for the honor because he embodied "USF's Jesuit Catholic mission, as a student, a member of the 1951 Dons' 'undefeated, untied and uninvited' football team, then as a beloved father, husband, longtime San Francisco educator, and well-known NFL linesman official." With the renaming of the residence hall, Toler's legacy is now even further solidified.

Charles Follis
Photo Credit to The College of Wooster

Chapter Two

The First Paid African-American Black Football Player

L ike a strong cyclone that tears through a region leaving destruction in its wake, **Charles Follis**, a legendary athlete nicknamed "*The Black Cyclone*" was so intimidating on the field, in 1899 he was hired and paid to play the sport, becoming the first paid Black football player when the game was born in Ohio.

Born of former slaves in Cloverdale, Virginia, like a strong storm, Follis was powerful, fast, nimble, and feared. He played with and against volunteers in various capacities because of his ability to play both offense and defense. In 1902, before football was an organized and regulated sport, volunteer players entertained spectators by rolling around in the mud, punching, kicking, and sometimes biting each other for fun.

Years later, writer and football historian Jim Stoner brought early football escapes and Follis' story to life through the movie, *"The Black Cyclone."* Stoner wrote in the *Ohio Connection*:

"In 1901, Coach Frank Schiffer took his team from Shelby to play *The Wooster Athletic Association*. While Shelby was by far the dominant team, *Charles Follis was Wooster's star player*. Schiffer was so impressed by Follis's skill that he decided he'd rather have Follis play with his team, and immediately offered him $10.00 a game to move to Shelby, a "Sundown Town," and play for his Shelby Blues."

Fierce and Popular

The natural-born leader was voted team captain of the first-ever varsity Wooster High School Football team, earning this honor at a time when Black people couldn't eat or sleep in certain places. The right half-back organized and established a squad that had **no losses that year**.

Like a cyclone, he was a force of nature that tore through a stronghold. Follis played for Shelby during the 1902 and 1903 seasons. During a 58–0 win over a team from Fremont, Follis ran for a 60-yard touchdown. In 1904, Follis helped lead the *Shelby Blues* to an 8–1–1 record. The Blues' only loss was to the 1904 *Ohio League Champions*.

In 1906, the Blues became an entirely open professional team. Due to an injury, Charles missed the early part of the season. He did however return in the second half of the season.

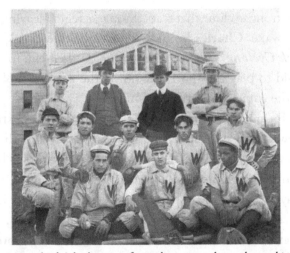

Charles Follis sitting (right) looks away from the camera lens when taking a photo with The College of Wooster baseball team. Photo Credit to The College of Wooster

He earned many trophies during his college football career. The "Black Cyclone" earned one of the greatest gridiron names in the 1900s while playing for the amateur team, *Wooster Athletic Association*. In 1904, Follis signed a contract with the *Shelby Athletic Club*, later the *Shelby Blues*. With that contract, he became **the first professional African-American football player.**

Laying the Groundwork for Jackie Robinson

Follis played on the team with Branch Rickey, a close friend and a Ohio Wesleyan University student and future Brooklyn Dodger owner who would sign Jackie Robinson to integrate major league baseball in 1947. Rickey never forgot Follis, recalling the *"ability, talent, and character of Charles Follis,"* when he sought out recruiting a player like him. For that reason, Follis is credited with the inspiration to integrate "America's Game" and changed sports and the country forever.

Racial Discrimination

Volunteer players would play dirty throughout all four quarters of the game which lasted about 12 to 15 minutes a quarter. But **"The Black Cyclone"** was subjected to harsher treatment than his teammates. The descendant of former slaves, Follis endured verbal racial comments. He was also kicked with football cleats and pushed with the balling of fists while laying underneath the pile in a defenseless mode.

That kind of brutality would test the patience and temperament of the most tolerant athlete. Follis, who came from a large family with many siblings, would hold his own using his impressive 6'0 foot, 200-pound frame to plow past other players.

According to the website *Black Past:*

"At a game in Toledo in 1905, fans taunted him with racial slurs until the Toledo team captain addressed the crowd and asked them to stop. In Shelby, Follis joined his teammates at a local tavern after a game; the owner denied him entry."

Career-ending Injury

At the Thanksgiving Day game of the 1906 season, Follis suffered a career-ending injury.

Death and Extensive Injuries

Jim Stoner, who carefully researched Follis further described the brutal sport this way, "This occurred at a time in history when football was extremely dangerous–**16 people died each year playing the sport in Ohio (1902-1906).** President Teddy Roosevelt, if not for some critical changes in the game, threatened to ban football altogether."

On Thanksgiving Day 1906, while playing against the *Franklin Athletic Club of Cleveland*, the star athlete suffered another injury that would end his football career.

A Baseball Career

Follis left football and Shelby in 1902 to play baseball in *The Negro Leagues of Baseball*, barnstorming for the superstar *"Cuban Giants."*

Sadly, Follis's career ended sooner than expected, but he did not fall to injury on the field. The once seemingly impenetrable mass of energy succumbed to pneumonia in 1910. He was only 31.

The Follis Legacy

Follis' legacy didn't end when he died. His legacy continues down the "way" a good bit. You can drive down a street in the city of Shelby named **Charles Follis Way** and shop, dine, sip coffee, and visit with friends along the newly renamed street and then follow the **Charles Follis Trail** around town.

The "Way" in Charles Follis's Way is symbolic of more than a street or avenue but rather symbolizes the way one can go to follow in Follis's footsteps.

"By honoring Follis, Shelby is joining efforts around the nation to reject the racism that was common throughout our history," Jim Stoner told *The Richland Source* in October 2020. Shelby Mayor Steven Schag called the move, "yet another step on the path to healing ills of the past."

At the ceremony, Schag remembered Follis as a man who left his mark on the world. "He has left a legacy for the ages, not merely as a football player but as a man of character and class." Follis never did see how he influenced history and the future trajectory of the sport. But his descendants did. Another newspaper account in the Shelby Daily Globe shows Follis's niece and great-niece proudly posing for pictures with Mayor Shag at the street sign dedication ceremony.

The mayor recalled that Follis's speed and skill as a running back earned him the nickname **The Black Cyclone** but it was his strength of character that helped him fend off racial injustice and prejudice with strength and dignity.

Shelby Mayor Steven Schag:

"*The 'Way'* means a method or a manner of doing something. And we're here today to honor the **Charles Follis Way** -- *the way* he modeled faith and fortitude. *The way* he handled the pressure and pain of racially charged indignities that came his way and *the way* he played with professionalism and passion. *The way* he showed poise and class on and off the field."

A high school stadium called Follis Field, a Follis scholarship, and Follis Way is named after the outstanding athlete as is a walking/exercise trail.

The Black Cyclone Trail has 9 stops which include Charles Follis's boyhood home, the schools he attended, and even travels past his former workplace. It ends at the Follis family gravesite and the Charles Follis Memorial Stone.

Charles Follis Day

Charles Follis Day in the state of Ohio is recognized on February 3rd, what would have been his birthday. The holiday became official when Governor John Kasich signed it into law in 2018.

It was more than a hundred years ago on September 16, 1904, when Follis signed a contract with Shelby making him the first Black man contracted to play professional football on an integrated team. A talented duel-athlete, soon after he also became the first Black catcher to move from college baseball into the Negro Leagues.

In Canton, Ohio a plaque with Charles Follis's name resides at The Professional Football Hall of Fame. It recognizes him as the first Black professional football player.

Charles Follis sitting (left) wears a black hat and looks down while the photographer snaps this photograph with The College of Wooster baseball team. Photo Credit to The College of Wooster

Born of a farm laborer, Charles' love of the game during his brief life blew through the new sport like a cyclone tearing up a field. **The Black Cyclone** displayed tenacity that helped him overcome many trials and racial barriers on the field and off before his untimely death in 1910. A trailblazer in the African-American community and a sports legend among fellow football players, historians, and enthusiasts, Charles Follis is inspiring future generations of aspiring athletes.

"I've often said that Shelby has a storied past with a bright future," said Mayor Schag. "It's very inspiring to see where we've come from. In that story, the life of Charles Follis is truly one of the bright gems."

Chapter Two Timeline

Charles W. Follis

The Black Cyclone

- **Born:** February 3, 1879, Cloverdale, Virginia
- **Died:** April 5, 1910, at the age of 31
- **Position:** Halfback
- **Sports:** Football and Baseball
- **Height:** 6 feet 0 in (1.83 m)
- **High School:** Wooster, OH (Wooster HS)
- **College:** Wooster College
- **Professional:** Wooster Athletic Association (1901) and Shelby Blues of the "Ohio League" from (1902-1906).
- **Career Awards:** First Black professional football player and first Black catcher to play in the Negro Leagues.
- **Parents:** Catherine Matilda Anderson Follis and James Henry Follis. They had seven children together. Charles was probably the third born of seven children. The older siblings were Lelia M.(b. 1874) and Cora Belle (b. 1876). Sister Laura Alice was born in 1880 and Brother Curtis W. was born in 1884 and died at the young age of 19 in 1903. In 1885, the family moved to Wooster, Ohio where Walter Joseph (b. 1888) and Lucy Jane (b. 1890) were born.

Accomplishments and Timeline

1879: Charles W. Follis was born on February 3, 1879, to James Henry and Catherine Matilda Anderson Follis in Cloverdale, Virginia. Catherine Matilda (b. 1848-d.1922) and James Henry (b.1846 –d. 1910). Charles W. Follis' father was a farm laborer.

1899: In 1899, as a junior in high school, Charles helped organize the school's first varsity football team. His schoolmates elected him captain.

1901: Follis entered Wooster College, in 1901, however, he chose to play football for the amateur Wooster Athletic Association, rather than the college team. As a member of the WAA team, he earned the nickname of the "**Black Cyclone from Wooster.**"

1902: In 1902, Frank C. Schieffer, manager of the Shelby Athletic Club secured employment for Follis at Howard Seltzer and Sons Hardware Store in rural Shelby, Ohio. The six-foot, 200-pound Follis played for Shelby in 1902 and 1903. Follis becomes the first Black professional American football player.

1903: Branch Rickey played against Follis on October 17, 1903, when he ran for a 70-yard touchdown against the Ohio Wesleyan football team.

1904: Follis helped the Blues to an 8-1-1 record. On September 16, 1904, Follis signed a contract with Shelby making him the first Black man contracted to play professional football on an integrated team. He was also the first Black catcher to move from college baseball into the Negro Leagues. Follis played on the team with Branch Rickey, the Ohio Wesleyan University student and future Brooklyn Dodger owner who would sign Jackie Robinson to integrate major league baseball in 1947.

1905: Like other players who integrated sports teams, Follis faced discrimination. Players on opposing teams targeted Follis with a rough play that resulted in injuries. At a game in Toledo in 1905, fans taunted him with racial slurs until the Toledo team captain addressed the crowd and asked them to stop. In Shelby, Follis joined his teammates at a local tavern after a game; the owner denied him entry.

1906: At the Thanksgiving Day game of the 1906 season, Follis suffered a career-ending injury. Follis turned to baseball, a sport he played for many years in the spring and summer. Having played for Wooster College and in the Ohio Trolley League, Follis was an experienced baseball player, but could only play in segregated baseball leagues. He played for the Cuban Giants, a Black baseball team, as a catcher.

1910: On April 5, 1910, at the age of 31, Follis died of pneumonia in Cleveland, after playing in a Cuban Giants game. He was buried in Wooster Cemetery in Wooster, Ohio.

1975: While Follis' professionalism was reported by the local press, his role as the first Black professional football player was not known by sports historians until many years later. In 1975, researchers rediscovered halfback Follis' on-the-field achievements while reviewing old pages of the *Shelby Daily Globe*, to locate evidence that Follis had played as a professional. After hours of examining the tattered newspapers, researchers finally came across an article in the September 16, 1904 edition that announced Follis had signed a contract for the upcoming season.

1998: In 1998, the football field/outdoor track facility at Wooster High School, Follis Field, was dedicated in his honor.

2013: In August 2013, a play named *"The Black Cyclone"* was put on at the Malabar Farm State Park in Lucas, Ohio. The script was written by an area playwright, Jim Stoner. The story relives Follis' life, football career, and family. In the same year, Follis was inducted into the College of Wooster Hall of Fame.

Henry McDonald in his baseball uniform for the
Pittsburgh Colored Stars, no date available.
Photo credit & Courtesy of: Historic Geneva

Chapter Three

First Haitian Black Professional American Football Player

When Henry McDonald was born on August 31, 1890, in impoverished Port-au-Prince, Haiti, his parents wanted a better life for him. At the tender age of five years old, his father and mother allowed an American banana and coconut importer to adopt him and bring him to Canandaigua, New York. His parents hoped that their son would be able to get a good education and have a better life in the United States.

"He was my father's boss and just took a liking to me," McDonald recalled. "My natural parents realized it was a great opportunity for me to go to America".

Sure enough, McDonald became the best-known Black professional player in the pre-NFL years. But that opportunity came at a high price.

"I didn't see my mother again for over *55 years* when I took my family back to Haiti for a visit."

First Black to Graduate from Rochester, N.Y.'s East High School

Henry McDonald spent his early childhood in Canandaigua, New York. His family then moved to the Finger Lakes region in New York, allowing McDonald to become the **first Black person to graduate from**

— 29 —

Rochester's East High School. He was an outstanding football and baseball player for Rochester East High and Canandaigua Academy. He stood out as a competitive athlete in both sports. McDonald played during a time when much of America was still segregated and before the NFL was formed.

Motorcycle McDonald

Young McDonald possessed the ability to run at lightning-fast speeds. His quickness earned him the nickname, "**Motorcycle McDonald.**" McDonald said he could run 100 yards in *10.2 seconds*. The world record at the time for running the 100-yard dash was 10 seconds flat. Motorcycle McDonald darted at Olympic speeds as a running back. This talent led him to become one of the first Black men to play professional football.

Playing football was a dirty and tough sport back then. Motorcycle McDonald played in the sandlots. Both his helmet and football cleats were made of leather. He didn't play on turf football fields and didn't use state-of-the-art equipment as the players do today. He played under much more difficult conditions but did so because he loved the game of football.

A flashy half-back, McDonald began his professional career in 1911 with the *Rochester Jeffersons, New York Colored Giants,* and the *Pittsburgh Colored Stars*. Rochester Jeffersons' owner Leo Lyons, after being amazed at McDonald's speed, enticed him to play for his team.

$15/day for two games a day

Throughout his professional career, McDonald had a hard time making ends meet by playing football. He never took home more than $15 a day and to bring that amount home he had to play two exhausting games. He enjoyed playing halfback *since running backs received the highest pay on the team.*

He told reporters that *he often passed a hat around at halftime for* **donations** *from spectators.*

He would take a trolley to Canandaigua to play for the town team in the afternoon after he played the morning game in Rochester for the Jeffersons.

Discrimination: Black is Black; White is White

During his 7 seasons of playing professional football (between 1911 and 1917), McDonald only recalled one negative racial incident. McDonald and an All-Syracuse team traveled to Ohio to meet the Jim Thorpe-led Canton Bulldogs. The trouble began when Canton's Earle "Greasy" Neale threw McDonald out of bounds and made his feelings concerning the Black player quite clear.

McDonald told the *Democrat and Chronicle* that Pro Football Hall of Famer Greasy Neale knocked him out of bounds, cocked his fist, and said, "Black is Black, and White is White where I come from and the two don't mix."

McDonald, an accomplished boxer, stood ready to answer Neale's challenge when Jim Thorpe unexpectedly intervened.

"We're here to play football," McDonald recalled Thorpe sternly telling his teammate, preventing a potential fight and drawing strong boundaries.

McDonald told the *Democrat and Chronicle* that Jim Thorpe's word was the law on the field. McDonald never remembered having any trouble with Neale or any other Canton player after that incident.

McDonald left the Jefferson football team after his 1917 season.

Baseball

Like other athletes at the time, Henry McDonald also played baseball. Henry played for seven years in baseball's Negro Leagues for the *Cuban Giants* and the *Pittsburgh Colored Stars*. He later became an athletic trainer at *Hobart College*, which is located in the heart of New York State's Finger Lakes Region.

Henry started the football program at *DeSales High School* and later coached young players at the school. By doing so, McDonald made history, becoming the **first Black American to serve as a head football coach in New York**. McDonald served as a coach at DeSales for 6 years (from 1937 until 1943.) **Motorcycle McDonald broke the color barrier again by becoming one of the first umpires when Little League was organized.**

Geneva's Little League Park is named in his honor. Motorcycle McDonald's impact on sports was so significant, that he became a charter member of the **Black Athletes Hall of Fame,** along with Willie Mays, Jackie Robinson, Jim Brown, and 34 others.

1941 DeSales High School football team from the 1941 yearbook.
Photo credit to & Courtesy of Historic Geneva

Today's Black athletes star in significant numbers on every NFL team, but it wasn't always that way in pro football, however, and it probably wouldn't be that way today if not for the handful of Black athletes of the pre-NFL years. **These early pioneers demonstrated fearlessness, character, and hard work and provided the first swipe at the invisible opponent, prejudice.**

In 1977, Geneva's mayor Helen Manley told the *Democrat and Chronicle* that Henry McDonald was a *"respected and beloved community citizen."* Even though his contributions to the sporting world were significant, *Rochester Sports* columnist Scott Pitoniak observed, "Even the most die-hard Rochester sports fan, they would probably not know who the heck he was."

But now, YOU know who Haitian-import Motorcycle Henry McDonald was!

Henry McDonald with Dr. John Stelter on Seneca Street in February 1967.
Photo credit to & Courtesy of Historic Geneva

Henry McDonald in umpire uniform from DeSales High School.
Photo credit to & Courtesy of Historic Geneva

Headshot of Henry McDonald by photographer PB Oakley, May 1953
Photo credit to Courteous of Historic Geneva

Chapter Three Timeline

Henry McDonald

Motorcycle McDonald

- **Born**: 1890 in Port-au-Prince, Haiti
- **Died**: 1976
- **Position:** Half-back
- **Sport:** Football, Baseball
- **High School**: Rochester, New York East High School & Canandaigua Academy
- **Professional:** Oxford Pros & Rochester Jeffersons
- **Nickname:** Motorcycle McDonald
- **Parents:** Adopted

Accomplishments and Timeline

1890: Henry C. McDonald was born in Port-au-Prince, Haiti.

1908: McDonald became the First Black Haitian American to graduate from Rochester's East High School

1911: McDonald began playing professional football for the Oxford Pros. In the same year, Henry earned the nickname, **"Motorcycle McDonald"** because of his ability to run so fast. In addition, later that year he played for the Rochester Jeffersons.

1917: McDonald and the Jeffersons (playing under the guise of the "Syracuse 47th Infantry") traveled to Ohio to play the Canton Bulldogs, led by Jim Thorpe. Trouble began when Canton's Greasy Neale threw McDonald out of bounds and snapped, "Black is Black and White is White where I come from and the two don't mix."

1918: Henry played seven years in baseball's Negro Leagues for the Cuban Giants and the Pittsburgh Colored Stars.

1919: McDonald was inducted into the inaugural class of the Geneva (New York) Sports Hall of Fame. Henry was also a charter member of the Black Athlete's Hall of Fame, along with baseball superstars, Willie Mays,

Jackie Robinson, and one of the greatest running backs of all times, if not the greatest, legendary professional NFL player, Jim Brown.

1937: Henry was named the head football coach at DeSales High School, making him the **first Black Haitian American to serve as a high school football coach in New York State.**

1939: Henry McDonald was one of the First Black American umpires when Little League was organized in 1939.

1976: McDonald was honored by the **Pro Football Hall of Fame** as one of the **Football Black American Pioneers** decades after he died.

2007: Geneva's Little League Park in Geneva, New York is named in his honor.

Gideon Smith Portrait
circa 1916
Photo courtesy of MSU Archives and Historical Collections.

Chapter Four

One of the First Black African-Americans to play College Football

Gideon Edward Smith was born in Northwest Norfolk County, Virginia, on July 13, 1889, just 24 years after the abolition of slavery. He is sometimes referred to by the name G.E. The name Gideon in Hebrew means **Great Warrior**. To football historians, the name may have the same meaning.

In 1910, this fierce athlete graduated from *Hampton Institute*. In that same year, he enrolled in *Ferris Institute*, where he played football, was the first African-American to do so, and participated in the band. He is widely credited as being one of the first African-American students at Ferris Institute at a time when red carpets didn't welcome African-Americans. In 1912, Gideon left the Ferris Institute to continue his college football career at *Michigan Agricultural College (MAC)*, which is today known as *Michigan State University*.

Gideon Smith came there to play football for the MAC Aggies and focus on his education. He tried to join the team as a freshman, however, Aggies coach John Macklin turned him away by not giving him a team uniform. Smith was determined to play so he borrowed some of his high-school gear from one of his classmates and then showed up to practice daily.

Macklin was impressed with his tough playing on the football field. He allowed him to stay on the team.

In 1913, he became the school's **first Black American varsity football student-athlete to participate in any sports at the University.** Lyman

Frimodig, a former MSU administrator and historian said, "I never saw a better tackle."

As a sophomore, on October 11, 1913, Smith's team faced off against Michigan, which would be their biggest and toughest competitor. The Aggies were no match for the Michigan Wolverines. Before this game as they dominated them on their first seven match-ups and gave them three goose eggs of shutouts of 39-0, 46-0, and 119-0. The Aggies jumped out in front of the Wolverines with a 12-0 lead, with the help of Smith who played tackle. They were the first team to beat Michigan, 12-7, and finish the year undefeated. This was the school's first-ever victory over the University of Michigan.

The Detroit Press notices

In 1913, the *Detroit Press* noted the game between the Michigan Agriculture College Aggies and the University of Michigan Wolverines *was "among the biggest upsets in college football history."*

Smith was acknowledged by the school as the first Black tackle ever at MAC. G.E. played for the University for two years from 1913 to 1915. The determined tackle accumulated a 17-3 record. His offense outscored their opponents by a huge margin of 636-123.

He was acknowledged and celebrated as the **First African-American student-athlete at Michigan State**. He had an efficacious career at MAC and received a warm letter of congratulations in 1913 from Woodbridge N. Ferris, then the Governor of Michigan. The letter was widely published in several newspapers.

Below is Governor Ferris' Letter to Gideon Smith:

"My Dear Mr. Smith:

I have been watching the reports of the M. A. C. football team. I am glad that you are receiving the same consideration at M.A.C. that you received at Ferris Institute. I am glad that merit counts.

I want to congratulate you upon the splendid work you have been doing on the football team. Your friends at the Ferris Institute read of your success with delight.

I like you for two reasons: First because you are a man and you have a wholesome ambition for doing your work well. Second, I like you because you are a success in football. Go ahead. I am sure that you are now realizing in a measure your ambition, and I am also sure that the future is rich with promise for you. I congratulate M.A.C. upon having a man of your ability on their team, a man who reflects credit upon himself and upon his fellow associates.

With best wishes, I remain, as ever.

Cordially yours
WOODBRIDGE N. FERRIS, Governor.
(*New York Age*, February 12, 1914)"

Praise for the Chocolate-Hued member of the Michigan Aggies

The *Detroit Tribune* also heaped praise upon the man they referred to as "*the chocolate-hued member of the Michigan Aggies*" claiming that he (despite his Black skin) "vied with the best of them for popularity among the farmers." His football skills certainly merited admiration. According to *Ferris State University's Jim Crow Museum website*, Smith starred on both sides of the football. "On offense, he was a superior blocker; on defense, he was a rugged and powerful tackler."

Of All-American Class

In 1915, *The Daily News of Chicago* noticed Smith's significant contributions to the game:

"Smith, playing his last year for the Michigan Aggies, is another wonderful tackle. Coaches Harper of Notre Dame, Yost of Michigan, and Stehm of Nebraska, all of whom have played against him, unite in declaring him of All-American class."

Macklin, his coach, has little to say about him, summing up his opinion in these words: 'He is the greatest tackle I ever saw, East or West. The big colored man was largely responsible for the success of the Lansing team this year and was used offensively and defensively.'" (New York Age, December 23, 1915).

Smith's Shining Moment

The man whose name means "Great Warrior" had a shining moment in his professional career. It came in Akron on Oct. 31, 1914 when the team he was playing against. After recovering a fumble on the Aggie goal line, Smith scooped up the ball and took off down the middle of the field. It appeared as if he was going to take it until he was pulled down a few yards shy of the end zone. Smith's fumble scamper of 95 yards registers longer than any other player in program history.

A portion of the headline in the *Saginaw Courier-Herald* referenced the Warrior Smith run the following day:

"Negro Lineman Furnishes Thrill with Sprint for 95-Yard Gain."

Later in the same game, Smith ripped off a 60-yard sprint for the score adding to the 75-6 outcome.

Last African-American to play professional football before the birth of the NFL in 1920

After Smith graduated from college in the spring of 1916, he went on to a short but successful pro career. The Canton Bulldogs signed him for one year. He played alongside the legendary Jim Thorpe with the Canton Bulldogs and played a vital role in the team's success. In the same year, Canton went on to win the League Championship with the help of a phenomenal play by Smith. In the team's final game against bitter rival Massillon, he recorded a crucial fumble recovery to help preserve the Championship and the 6-0 victory of the Tigers.

Smith was the last African-American to play professional football entirely before the establishment of the National Football League.

Smith enlisted in the United States Military

After he graduated from MAC in 1916, Smith was named Commander of Cadets and also served as a chemical science instructor at *West Virginia Collegiate Institute*, which is today known as *West Virginia State University* according to *1916 The Institute Monthly*. In 1919, Smith was the head football coach of the *Virginia Normal and Industrial Institute*, which today is known as *Virginia State University*.

In 1921, Smith returned to *Hampton Institute* to become the head football coach, a position he held until 1940, compiling a 102-44-12 record, including six one-loss seasons and two undefeated seasons in 1926 and 1931. His 1931 team outscored opponents 187 to 6 according to the College Football Data Warehouse.

His successful college career was ultimately recognized. Smith was inducted into *the Michigan State Athletics Hall of Fame* in 1992. According to Hampton University Athletics, he was inducted into the *Hampton Athletics Hall of Fame* in 2009 and Smith was named the American Football Coaches Association's recipient of the **2014 Trailblazer Award**. That award was created to honor early coaches at historically Black colleges and universities.

Smith truly was a trailblazer, the first African-American to play football at two different institutions and one of the first to play professional football. He was not just a football player; he also held teaching positions at two institutions and had a stellar career as a coach. Smith proved to many what a man can do when allowed to succeed. Ferris State is proud of what Gideon Smith accomplished and that their founder, Woodbridge Ferris, was one of the people who believed in Gideon and allowed him to succeed.

In 2015, Ferris State University Vice President for Diversity and Inclusion David Pilgrim tasked Media Specialist Franklin Hughes found photographs of Ferris State graduate Gideon Smith. Hughes found evidence that dozens of African-American students originating at Hampton Institute subsequently enrolled at Ferris Institute. The Ferris State founder and then-president Woodbridge N. Ferris offered opportunity to Southern African-American students of the era at his school, then Ferris Institute. Here's why that's unusual. Hampton Institute's coursework would have prepared students for manual labor, which was considered appropriate work for African Americans in the Jim Crow South. But Ferris Institute offered training related to fields such as business and healthcare, an opportunity Gideon Smith embraced.

Gideon Smith served time for his country in World War I. After being in the war, in 1921, he journeyed to Virginia and to Hampton Institute (now known as Hampton University), where he not only worked as a professor of physical education but served as the head football coach as well. This former commander of cadets remained in the head coach position for the next two decades for a total of 20 years. The program captured its first Black college national championship, with a 5-1 record in his second year as head coach in 1922. Following the national championship season, the Pirates went on to win four more conference championships. Smith had an impressive 102-44-12 record, including six one-loss seasons and two undefeated seasons in 1926 and 1931. His 1931 team outscored opponents an impressive 187 to 6. After his coaching career at Hampton Institute finished in 1942, he continued to excel as a professor and assistant athletics director until his retirement in 1955. Thirteen years later, he died at the age of 78.

Discrimination

John Milton Belcher III remembered his grandfather fondly and with a great deal of respect.

Belcher said: "I remember my grandfather as the most gentle person I've encountered in my life. I honestly never saw him angry, never saw him express any kind of irritation or impatience. That is something I truly continue to reflect upon, as I grew into adulthood because I still find it almost unfathomable knowing his story and knowing his journey."

Before he left East Lansing, a group of area fans awarded Gideon Smith with a gold watch and told him it was for the courage he showed in enduring hostility on and off the field because of the color of his skin.

His grandson recalled:

"I'm trying to still wrap my head and my heart around how he could emerge from the types of challenges he faced, from all of his myriad encounters with racism, from the injustices that he encountered from all of the indignities, large and small, with that gentle nature intact, and the sense of humanity he had, the willingness to help, and the kind of differences he made in other's lives. That remains a huge question for me and an inspiration."

Gideon Smith was born only 24 years after slavery ended. Yet his determination and his passion for football drove him forward despite the obvious and subtle obstacles he faced.

The Other Gideon Smith

The last Black to play exclusively during the pre-NFL years was Gideon "Charlie" Smith. It could be said of Smith that during his pro career, he was the most important man on the field for his team. Smith, a tackle, played just one game – and only as a late fourth-quarter substitute – for the 1915 Canton Bulldogs. However, during his brief pro appearance, he made a game-saving fumble recovery that not only preserved a 6-0 Canton advantage over arch-rival Massillon Tigers but assured the Canton aggregation of the "State Championship" resulting from the win.

Chapter Four Timeline

Gideon Smith

Chocolate-hued member of the Michigan Aggies

- **Born:** July 13, 1889, Norfolk County, Virginia
- **Died:** May 6, 1968
- **Position:** Tackle
- **College:** Michigan State University
- **Professional:** Michigan Agricultural
- **Career Awards:** 5 CIAA Football Championship (1922, 1925-1926, 1928, 1931)

Accomplishments

1910: Gideon Smith graduates from Hampton Institute.

1911: Smith enrolled into Ferris Institute.

1912: Gideon enrolled into Michigan Agricultural College (MAC), which is today known as Michigan State University.

1913: Smith received congratulations letter from governor, Woodbridge N. Ferris.

1915: Detroit Tribune referred to Smith as "the Chocolate-hued member of the Michigan Aggies."

1916: Smith graduates from MAC and was named Commander of Cadets and served as a chemical science instructor at West Virginia Collegiate Institute, which is known today as West Virginia State University.

1919: Smith was the head football coach of the Virginia Normal and Industrial Institute, today known as Virginia State University.

1921: Smith returned to Hampton Institute to become the head football coach, a position he held until 1940, compiling a 102-44-12 record, including six one-loss seasons and two undefeated seasons in 1926 and 1931.

1992: Smith was inducted into Michigan State Athletics Hall of Fame, being tabbed as a "Warrior of his time."

2009: Gideon was inaugurated into Hampton Athletics Hall of Fame.

2014: Smith was named the American Football Coaches Association's recipient of the Trailblazer Award. That award was created to honor early coaches at historically black colleges and universities.

Chapter Five

Fritz Pollard: First Black Coach in the National Football League

Nicknamed the **Human Tornado, Fritz Pollard** was considered one of the **most influential African-American athletes in American history.**

"Football isn't a game; It's a *religion*," Pollard said.

Pollard's approach of treating football like a religion leads to many firsts. Pollard was the first African-American to play on a championship team at *Brown University* against *Harvard* and *Yale*, as well as the first known Black quarterback and coach.

"He's one of the greatest runners I've ever seen," legendary sportswriter Walter Camp said of Pollard.

After college, along with Bobby Marshall, Pollard was one of the first two African-Americans in the National League in 1920.

Pollard was the first Black player selected to the **Walter Camp All-American team**, the first to play in the **Rose Bowl** (1916) and the first Black to be inducted **into the National College Football Hall of Fame (1954).**

Pollard was posthumously inducted into the **NFL Hall of Fame** in 2005, the **Rose Bowl Hall of Fame** in 2015, and the **Fritz Pollard Alliance** - a group established to promote minority hiring in the NFL. The Fritz Pollard Alliance is named in Pollard's honor.

A life well-lived

On a hot sunny day in Canton, Ohio, Fritz Pollard's grandson, Fritz Pollard III, delivered a heartfelt message at his grandfather's enshrinement. The younger Fritz, who is named after his famous ancestor, addressed a crowd who had gathered around a bronze bust. Flanked by his brother, Fritz addressed the newly unveiled likeness of his namesake, Fritz Pollard I. He gestured to the bust of the pioneer and trailblazer.

"Grandpa," he said gesturing. "The crowds are *cheering*."

If Fritz was still alive he'd sport a broad, proud smile to go along with his easygoing demeanor. He blazed a trail in sports during a time when Black coaches were not noticed let alone celebrated. Pollard achieved what was then considered to be nearly impossible. He was chosen as the first Black to coach in NFL history.

His grandson gazed at the image of him when referenced the crowd.

"The seats behind me and in front of me are filled with your legacy. After today everyone will know the gifts you've given to football. From its earliest days from its crowd-thrilling game-winning plays to a string of firsts."

Pollard was the first to do many things as a Black college student. Pollard was the first to play in the Rose Bowl and enter the College Football Hall of Fame. Pollard qualified for Walter Camp's famous and prestigious All-American team. He became the first Black coach and quarterback. Fritz said that his grandfather did more than break barriers in sports. "And last but not least, pushing for African-American equality in pro leagues. You've more than earned your place in history in the history of football."

Racial Turmoil

In 1919, when the former Brown University All-American running back joined the Akron Pros, more than 25 race riots erupted in major U.S. cities. The Akron Pros was a pro football team that would later become a charter member of the NFL.

Pollard later reflected on those years. He said he was able to endure racial prejudice and hatred because his father taught him dignity and self-respect.

"My father had taught me that I was too big to be humiliated by prejudiced Whites. If I figured a hotel or restaurant didn't want me, I stayed away. I didn't go sniffing around hoping they'd accept me. I was never interested in socializing with Whites. I was there to play football and make my money."

Pollard's determination to oppose and surmount the odds led to his success in life. Brown University's website calls Pollard, "a true renaissance man." The narrative goes on to gush about how Pollard "broke barriers of every sort in the business and the entertainment industry, as well as in sports." Pollard excelled in every discipline. Who was this remarkable man? Let's learn more about the great Fritz Pollard.

Humble beginnings

Frederick Douglass "Fritz" Pollard, Sr, was born in Chicago, Illinois, on January 27, 1894. Pollard's mother, Catherine Amanda Hughs Pollard, a seamstress, was Native American, and his father, John William Pollard, a barber, an African-American who boxed professionally during the Civil War.

Inspired by social reformer Frederick Douglass, Pollard's parents named their son Frederick after hearing the preacher speak the preceding year. Pollard attributed much of his success in life to his ancestors who demonstrated dedication, hard work, endurance, faith, courage, and a pioneering spirit.

Fritz grew up in Rogers Park, Illinois, a largely White suburb of Chicago. They were the first Black family to settle in the all-White "village" of Rogers Park. The seventh of eight children, they called him Fred, but later the nickname "Fritz" came from the residents in the neighborhood. It was a name that stuck with him throughout life.

Pollard attended Albert G. Lane Manual Training High School in Chicago, also known as Lane Tech. In an NFL interview, Fritz talked about his brother saying, "Where is my kid brother? You have not given him a chance to play. I am not going to play because you have not given my kid brother a chance to play."

Fritz admitted that advocating by his brother helped. "Because of my brother, they gave me a chance to play on the Lane Tech football team at 89 pounds."

According to biography.jrank.org, Fritz Pollard was a highly successful football and track athlete even during his high school years. Fritz was an all-around athlete, excelling as a running back, a three-time Cook County track champion, and a talented baseball player.

After graduation from Lane Tech, Pollard went on to play college football briefly for Dartmouth, Northwestern, and Harvard before receiving a scholarship from the Rockefeller family to play for Brown University.

A distinguished career at Brown University; Racism; Respect

Among his many honors, Pollard was the first African-American to be elected into the National College Football Hall of Fame as well as the recipient of an honorary doctorate from Brown University. Along with his amazing athletic ability and accomplishment, Pollard was a courageous advocate for confronting racial barriers and creating opportunities for African-Americans, both in the athletic and business world.

1918 Fritz served as Physical Director of the YMCA unit at Camp Meade, Maryland.
Photo credit to: Brown University Library

Fritz went to Brown University and majored in chemistry. Pollard broke color barriers by becoming the first Black football player at Brown.

According to Fritz Pollard III, his grandfather had to prove himself. "His teammates, basically, really wouldn't talk to him or anything until they saw what he could do."

What Pollard could do was rack up yards, 60, 70, and 80 yards at a time. Once he got the ball, the tough 5-foot-9 halfback flew downfield, his trademark baggy football pants flapping in the breeze.

"Once they saw his **talent,** he won them over," Pollard III says.

"And his **personality** won them over. So from then on, they had his back no matter what."

That would be useful. As the only African-American on the field, Pollard was the subject of verbal abuse and worse. In a 1915 college game, kicking and eye-gouging at the bottom of the pig pile were routine. Pollard was often a target.

"He learned how to protect himself by rolling over and kicking his feet like a cat if somebody tried to pile on and drag their feet on him to cut him," Pollard III says.

A report in a 1916 *New York Times* article reposted on the Brown University Website, said of Pollard's performance in a game between Brown University and Yale: "At every stage of this dazzling performance sturdy arms clad in blue yawned for him, but Pollard trickily shot out of their reach. Tacklers charged him fiercely enough to knock the wind out of any ordinary individual, but Pollard had the asset, which is the greatest to a football player-*He refused to be hurt.* It required a terrific shock to upset him. An ordinary tackle did nothing more than make him swerve slightly out of his course."

Pollard Received Death Threats

Seeing his value to the team, his teammates protected him.

"They would wear baggy uniforms, so that way no one could tell in the game who he was," Pollard III said. "And sometimes they even darkened their faces with shoe polish, so they couldn't tell who he was."

"They had death threats when they played certain schools in certain areas. And these were Ivy League schools that still were racist as anywhere else. It went all through the country," Pollard III says.

"There were times when he had to be escorted onto the field by the police," said Dr. Stevens Towns, another of Fritz Pollard's grandsons.

Towns recalled, "Yale fans used to sing "**Bye Bye Blackbird**" when Pollard came on the field."

When Brown University earned an invitation to the 1916 Rose Bowl, the New Year's Day game against Washington State University almost didn't happen. Pollard's grandsons recalled being told what happened at the team's hotel.

"They wouldn't let my grandfather sign in," Pollard III told everyone. "So they said, 'Well, take us back to the train station because if you won't let him stay, we're going back.' The team was prepared to go back to Rhode Island if they weren't going to let my grandfather stay in the hotel."

"The hotel worked it out," Towns said. "Meaning they let him stay."

Marriage and Divorce

In June 1914, Fritz Pollard Sr. married Ada Laing. They later divorced in 1940. He then married Mary Ellen Austin in 1947. The couple had three daughters: Leslie Keeling, Gwendolyn Burrel, and Eleanor Pollard Towns.

Mrs. Eleanor Towns who lived until her 98th year, lived in Indianapolis. She passed away on February 11, 2020. Born in Cleveland, Ohio, she was the last surviving daughter of Fritz Pollard. Mrs. Towns attended West Virginia State College and earned a bachelor's degree in Physical Education at George Williams College. In Chicago, IL. She was survived by her husband of 74 years, Dr. Clarence Towns, Jr.; a son, Dr. Stephen A. Towns and his wife Dr. Jeanette Sabir-Holloway) and their daughter, Stephany C. Towns as well as grandchildren, Damon Ellis, Jenae Holloway, and Geoffrey Holloway, and great-granddaughter, Zora Holloway according to the website tributearchive.com

Los Angeles Times

The L.A. Times wrote of Pollard on August 7, 2005, when Pollard's daughter, Eleanor Pollard Towns was interviewed by Sam Farmer for *"True Pioneer Gets His Due."* Towns told Farmer, "My father was a pioneer. They didn't use steroids back in those days, everything was raw talent. They did not make much money. They did it for the love of the game."

In a *Los Angeles Times* article, former Dallas Cowboys Calvin Hill reflected. **"Every player ought to be aware of Fritz Pollard and what he went through, especially every Black player,"** Hill worked as a team consultant. "There were a lot of people who stood up and fought, setting the stage for Blacks and Whites, good people to stand up and say, 'This is nonsense.' Today's players need to understand whose shoulders they're standing on and appreciate who helped them get where they are. **Fritz Pollard helped get them where they are."**

Discrimination

During his eight-year career, Pollard coached three other teams, Milwaukee, Hammond (Ind.), and Providence, and played quarterback for Hammond, another first for a Black player in the league.

Through it all, Pollard endured racism on and off the field. When he played for Akron, he dressed in a cigar shop that belonged to the team owner, then would be escorted to the game by police. He would arrive just before kickoff so he could minimize his interaction with the crowd.

Grandson, Fritz Pollard III, talked about how racism manifested itself. Some of his Brown teammates would paint their faces Black so fans would have a difficult time identifying him from a distance.

"As soon as he got the ball," his grandson said, "you knew who he was."

When Brown played at Yale things got especially ugly. As a pro, it wasn't uncommon for spectators to throw rocks and bottles at him, his daughter said. "He wouldn't let the people get the best of him," she said. "When people can't get your goat, they finally give in most of the time."

The Fritz Pollard Legacy

Fritz Pollard left a legacy and served to inspire the next generations toward greatness. According to *The L.A. Times*, Fritz Pollard Jr. (February 18, 1915 – February 15, 2003) was an athlete who competed for the United

States in the 1936 Summer Olympics in Berlin in the 110-meter hurdles where he won the bronze medal.

While a student at the University of North Dakota, Pollard Jr. was a running back for the football team. He was picked All North Central Conference in 1937 and 1938 and was Collier's Magazine Little All-America selection in football in 1938. Pollard graduated from UND with a bachelor's degree with a major in education. Pollard went on to earn a law degree from the John Marshall Law School. In addition, like his father, Pollard Jr. served in the U.S. Army as a special services officer during World War II. Some years after the war, Pollard Jr. became a Foreign Service officer and retired in 1981 as the director of the State Department's overseas school for U.S. citizens.

Fritz Pollard, running back for Brown University.
Photo credit to: John Hay Library, Brown University

Left to right: Fritz III, Fritz, Fritz Jr. Photo credit to: Brown University Library

Winning football from Nov. 18, 1916 game against Harvard,
21-0. Photo credit to: Brown University Library

Winning football from Nov. 11, 1916 game against Yale.
Photo credit to: Brown University Library

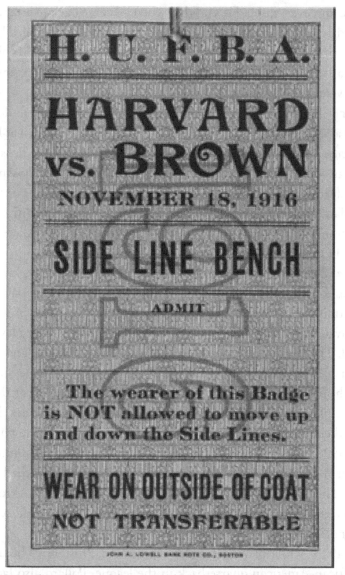

1916 Harvard vs. Brown sideline pass. Photo credit to: Brown University Library

Pollard Jr. is survived by one of his two children, Fritz D. Pollard III (Cheryl Pollard is deceased), and two grandchildren, Meredith Kaye Russell and Marcus Stephan Pollard.

In the article, *"Football legend "Fritz" Pollard"* by Kenan Heise, Pollard's daughter Leslie Kelling said, "My father was very easygoing and he was a brilliant man. People were just crazy about him. They tended to just give him everything. He said that when he came back in after a game, he found people had stuffed his locker full of money. They spoiled him. He was brilliant, but the only thing they cared about was his sports ability."

An article by Victor Okocha in *BlackPast* demonstrates what significant strides were made by Pollard.

"Once Pollard left Brown, Fritz shortly pursued a degree in dentistry, worked as a director for an Army YMCA, and coached football at Lincoln University. He later signed to play for the Akron (Ohio) Pros in the American Professional Football League (APFA) in 1919, following army service during World War I."

Pollard became the head football coach at Lincoln University in Pennsylvania and began playing professional football for Akron in the informal Ohio League in 1919.

Fritz was quoted in an interview as saying, "There was no knowledge of Professional football to amount to anything during those days. It was after I finished at Brown University. I went down to the University of Pennsylvania and I studied dentistry. They came to me about playing Pro football. That is how I happened to play against Jim Thorpe and some of his Indians. Naturally, I had heard about the great Jim Thorpe; I imagine he had heard of the great Fritz Pollard because I had a name at that time too. The players would look at me and call me different names. I would look at them and grin and then run for 80 yards for a touchdown."

In 1920, the Pros joined the newly founded American Professional Football Association, which later became the National Football League (NFL). The same year, Pollard was the star player for the Akron Pros, who won the first championship. Pollard continued to play and coach the NFL until 1926.

In 1923, while playing for the Hammond Pros, Fritz became the first African-American quarterback in the league. Pollard also facilitated integration in the NFL by recruiting other African-American players such as Paul Robeson, Jay Mayo Williams, and John Shelbourne and by organizing the first interracial all-star game featuring NFL players in 1922.

Pollard criticized Lincoln's administration, saying they had hampered his ability to coach and had refused to provide adequate travel accommodations for the team.

Letter from Team Manager Fred Ballou (1916), updating President Faunce on the team's preparations for the upcoming game. Photo credit to: Brown University Library

"Prior to the Hampton game, the team was compelled to go to Hampton by boat, sleeping on the decks and under portholes, " he told a reporter. "No cabins were provided, nor were they given a place to sleep after reaching Hampton. They lost the game through lack of rest."

Pollard also blamed the school for not providing the proper equipment. "I, myself, bought and paid $200 out of my pocket for football shoes for the team." He missed the 1920 Howard game, he said, because his Lincoln salary was so low that he was compelled to augment it with pay for Akron.

"It was evident in my first year at Akron back in 1919 they didn't want Blacks getting that money. There I was playing and coaching and pulling down the highest salary in pro football." Pollard told reporters.

In the YouTube video, *"Fritz Pollard, An Akron Legend/Lights Camera,"* Pollard admitted that he was a key member of the NFL's first Champion team, The Akron Pros, who posted a league-best of 8 wins, 0 losses, and 3 ties in the league in 1920. Fritz Pollard had 18 total touchdowns, 16 rushes, and 2 receptions. Pollard paved the pathway for the greats to be great. Fritz's presence in the league fundamentally changed the game for years to come. Pollard's contribution to the game and his legacy has shaped football into the game it is today.

Pollard coached four different teams in a single season

Fritz as Class Marshall at the 50th reunion of the Class of 1919. Photo credit to: Brown University Library

In 1921, the Pros named Pollard co-coach of the team, earning him the distinction of being the first African-American to coach in NFL History.

After becoming a coach for the NFL, Pollard was known to coach up to four different teams in a single season.

He also continued playing in the 1923 and 1924 seasons for an independent pro team in Pennsylvania called *The Coal League*. Then in 1928, he organized a professional all-African-American team in Chicago known as the Chicago Black Hawks. Playing against White teams around Chicago, the Black Hawks enjoyed great success and became a highly popular team until the Depression caused the team to fold in 1932.

Formed an Investment Firm; Ran a Coal Company; Served as Agent, Publisher; Producer; Promoter; Booking Agent; Tax Consultant

In addition to his athletic endeavors, Pollard was involved in several business enterprises. He began an **investment firm** that served the African-American community in 1922, and after its bankruptcy in 1931, he ran a **coal company** in New York and also served as a **casting agent** during the production of the 1933 film *Emperor Jones*.

From 1935 to 1942 Pollard **founded and operated** the *New York Independent News*, the first African-American tabloid newspaper, then in 1943 he **managed** *Suntan Studios* in Harlem, auditioning African-American entertainers called Soundies for the Soundies Distribution Corporation of America. The company was sold after World War II. In 1947 Pollard married Mary Ann Ellen.

Pollard was named to the **National College Football Hall of Fame,** in 1954, to named **R.I. Heritage Hall of Fame**, in 1967, named to **Brown Athletic Hall of Fame**, in 1971, named to **National Black Hall of Fame**, in 1973, and Brown University **honorary doctorate**, in 1981, named to **Pro Football Hall of Fame**, 2005.

Pollard's prophetic visit to the **Football Hall of Fame** *in Canton,
Ohio. Photo credit to: Brown University Library*

*Stadium view during 1916 game against Harvard, showing Pollard
nearing the goal line. The hay on the sidelines was to prevent the field
from freezing. Photo credit to: Brown University Library*

Following the sale of Soundies Distribution Corporation of America,
Pollard became a **booking agent** for nightclubs, radio, and television, and
eventually produced his movie in 1956 entitled *Rockin' the Blues*. The film,
similar to his music videos, featured new African-American artists.

From the 1950s-1975, when he retired, Pollard dedicated his time to
being a successful **tax consultant**. He died of pneumonia on May 11,
1986, in Maryland at the age of 92.

In 2005, he was finally inducted into the Pro Football Hall of Fame.

1915 Brown football team; Pollard was the only African-American
player on an Ivy League team during the 1915 football season.
Brown's opponents were less than gracious in their treatment of Pollard.
Photo credit to: Brown University Library

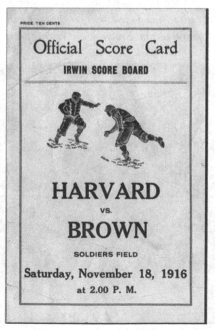

1916 Harvard vs. Brown official score card. Pollard was listed as right half back, #9.
Photo credit to: Brown University Library

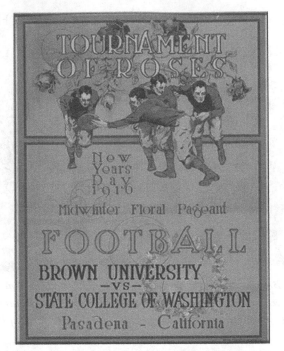

*Brown's 5-3-1 record for the 1915 season was modest. The 3-0 victory over Yale
proved to be the key to Brown's selection for the first annual Rose Bowl.
Photo credit to: Brown University Library*

*A special Pullman car carried the Brown contingent from
Providence to California and back.
Photo credit to: Brown University Library*

1916 Season
Following their appearance in the Rose Bowl,
expectations for the 1916 football season were high.
Relying on Pollard's skill, Brown swept through the first six games of
the season, surrendering only 3 points. The Bruins made history that
year by defeating both Yale and Harvard-the first team to do so in
the same season. Photo credit to: Brown University Library

1916 cartoon depicting Pollard's "wrath-like runs" in victory over Harvard.
Photo credit to: Brown University Library

Fritz (circled), known as "the human torpedo," nears Harvard's goal,
behind the blocking of team captain Mark Farnum.
Photo credit to: Brown University Library

"Brown-Collegiate Football Game
Thanksgiving Day, Nov. 30, 1916. Andrews Field, Providence, R.I."
(36" panoramic photo by K.K.N.E. F. A. George, Boston.)
Brown's rush for a second national title in 1916 was extinguished only
by its crushing 28-0 defeat at the hands of Colgate University on Andrews Field.
Photo credit to: Brown University Library

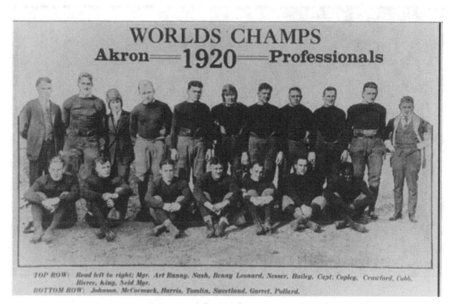

1914
Fritz's brother Leslie Pollard (standing, left) is Lincoln University's team coach.
An important role model for young Fritz, Leslie played football at Dartmouth
and was coaching at Lincoln University by the time Fritz graduated from
high school. Fritz followed in his footsteps to coach at Lincoln in 1918.
Photo credit to: Brown University Library

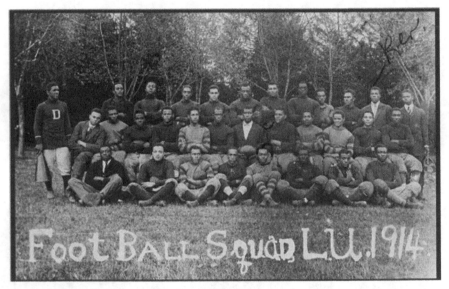

1920
Pollard on the bottom, right, with Akron Professionals.
The Pros were unbeaten and handed arch-rival, Jim Thorpe
and his Canton team had two shut-out losses.
Photo credit to: Brown University Library
Providence Steam Rollers (9) vs. Chicago Bears (6)
Professional Football-Braves Field, Boston, Dec. 9, 1925.
Pollard standing left of the pennant. (38 panoramic photos by General Studios,
Boston.) Pollard and Red Grange of the Bears were this game's principal gate
attractions, which the Steam Rollers won. Pollard was paid $500 for the game.
Photo credit to: Brown University Library

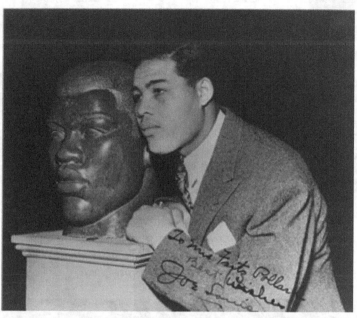

Pollard was the coach of the Brown Bombers, named after heavyweight boxing champion Joe Louis. Photo credit to: Brown University Library

Pollard with Brown teammates Bill Ormsby (left) and Jimmy Jermail (right) during 1946 reunion. Photo credit to: Brown University Library

Brown Rose Bowl Team reunion, taken in front of Sharpe Refectory.
The group had several reunions over the years, including a 40th
at the Rose Bowl with their 1916 opponents from Washington State.
Photo credit to: Brown University Library

An amateur musician himself,
Fritz Pollard was attracted to the Harlem nightclub scene
and was active in the Cotton Club.
Photo credit to: Brown University Library

*As a principal in Suntan Studios, Pollard created "soundies" to showcase
Black musicians. The film is most remembered for "Rockin the Blues" (1957)
a low-budget "race movie" that featured performances by F. E. Miller,
Connie Carroll, the Wanderers, the Harptones, the Hurricanes, and other
groups, interspersed with comic sequences by Mantan Moreland.
Photo credit to: Brown University Library*

*March 1959
Pollard in his New York office.
He put his promotional skills to work as a booking agent for Black musicians
and helped to launch the careers of many talented African-American artists.
Photo credit to: Brown University Library*

*During the 1950s, Fritz reconnoitered the field of politics with fellow Brown
alum John D. Rockefeller, Jr. (1897), and was a supporter of Nelson Rockefeller
and other Republican stalwarts, including Richard Nixon.
Because of Pollard's intercession, these politicians were able to make
important connections within the African-American community.
Photo credit to: Brown University Library*

*Pollard's activities in sports were not limited to football.
In the winter of 1917, after leaving Brown, he organized a touring Black basketball
team named the Providence Collegians, with Fritz as their captain and
guiding light-thus beginning his career as a promoter.
The scheduled game shown here against the Incorporators,
who billed themselves as "the colored champions," did not take place.
Photo credit to: Brown University Library*

*After retiring from football, Pollard became involved in the
entertainment industry in the 1950s and 1960s. As a theatrical agent,
Pollard booked Black talent in White clubs in New York.
Photo credit to: Brown University Library*

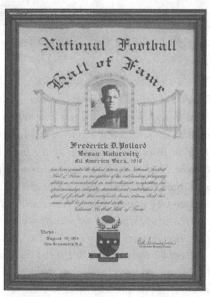

*Pollard was the first African-American elected
to the National College Football of Fame.
Photo credit to: Brown University Library*

*John ("Jay") Barry, Class of 1950, was instrumental in keeping
the Pollard legend alive. When Fritz was elected to the
National Collegiate Football Hall of Fame in 1954, Barry organized
"Fritz Pollard Day" at Brown to coincide with the induction ceremony.
As Brown's official football historian, Barry wrote extensively about Pollard in
the pages of the Brown Alumni Monthly, and, at the time he died in 1985, was
producing a book-length biography of Fritz Pollard and a documentary film
on Pollard's career. A friend of Fritz and the principal champion of his legacy,
it would seem that, twenty years after Barry's death, his lobbying efforts
have finally won Pollard his rightful spot in the Pro Football Hall of Fame.
J. Barry, Pollard's biographer, with Pollard on the steps of Brown Stadium
Photo credit to: Brown University Library*

Fritz Pollard Associates, INC.
PUBLIC RELATIONS CONSULTANTS
~~Circle 6-0885-6-7~~
NE.6-5081

288 Webster Ave.
New Rochelle,NY
November 1, 1969

~~GENERAL MOTORS BUILDING~~
~~1775 BROADWAY~~
~~New York 19, N.Y.~~

Dear Jay,

It was very kind of you to send me this copy of the
Brown Journal. Although I receive the booklet, I doubt very
much whether I would have looked through it enough to find
your story.

It takes a person like you who has had considerable
experience to write such a beautiful background of the
players you have picked for your all-time Brown Team, and I
was very **happy** to see that you had thought of me.

I will try to get up that way within the next 30 days.
Perhaps to see one of the games in November, at which time
we can sit down and have a chat.

I wish you would send a release of this story to Mr.
Jim O'Toole, c/o Standard Star - New Rochelle, N.Y.; also,
one to the Sports Editor of the Amsterdam News, 2340 - 8th
Avenue, New York, N.Y.

Were it not for fellows like you, I don't think that
much of the Heritage of Brown University would continue.

Coach Jardine is a fine young fellow; but no coach is
any good without players. I don't know who picks the players
for Brown University, but THEY (the players) picked are what
go to make up a good team, and then a coach just moulds them.

You know I coached pro-football, and when I had good
men, we won the World's Championship. Without them, we were
just good "runner ups."

Anyway, it was good hearing from you, and I had better
stop now or I will be writing your whole book for you.

Hoping to see you soon,

Regards,

Fritz

Fritz

*Letter from Pollard to J. Barry mentions his coaching philosophy:
"No coach is any good without players, the players picked are what go
to make up a good team, and then a coach just molds them."
Photo credit to: Brown University Library*

Pollard was inducted into the Brown University Athletic Hall of Fame in 1971.
Dr. Vernon Alden, Class of 1945, offers congratulations.
Photo credit to: Brown University Library

Chapter 5 Timeline

Frederick Douglass Fritz Pollard

The Human Tornado

- **Born:** January 27, 1874, Chicago, Illinois
- **Died:** May 11, 1986 (age 92)
- **Position:** Quarterback, Halfback, and Running back
- **Sports:** Football, baseball, and track
- **Height:** 5 ft. 9 in (1.75 m)
- **High School:** Chicago, IL (Lane Tech HS)
- **College:** Brown University
- **Professional as a player:** Akron Pros (1920-1921), Union Club of Phoenixville (1920), Milwaukee Badgers (1922), Gilberton Catamounts (Independent Pro Team) (1923-1924), Hammond Pros (1923, 1925), Providence Steam Roller (1925), Akron Indians (1925-1926)
- **Professional as a coach:** Lincoln (PA) (1918-1920), Akron Pros (1920-1921) and (1925-1926), Hammond Pros (1923 and 1925), the Providence Steam Roller (1925), and the Brown Bombers (1935-1938) and Chicago Black Hawks (1928)
- **Career Awards:** Fritz Pollard was the first Black African American head coach in the National Football League (NFL)
- **Parents:** Catherine Amanda Hughs Pollard (Native American) and John William Pollard (African American)
- **Married to Ada Laing and Mary Ella Austin:** Father of four children with his first wife, Ada Laing, they had one son and three daughters. They divorced in 1940, and he married Mary Ella Austin.

Accomplishments and Timeline

1874: Fritz Pollard was born in Chicago, Illinois. He grew up in Rogers Park, Illinois, a largely white suburb of Chicago. They were the first Black family to settle in the all-white "village" of Rogers Park. The seventh of eight children, young Fritz experienced racism and learned from his family how to pick his battles and subdue his emotions to achieve his goals in a predominantly White world.

1912: Graduated from Lane Technical High School with the class of 1912 and is named Lane Tech's Unsung Hero.

1914: Married Ada Laing

1916: Fritz Pollard was the first African-American from Brown University to play in the Rose Bowl. Nicknamed the "Human Torpedo," Pollard was credited for almost single-handedly beating both Yale and Harvard in the same week scoring 6 touchdowns and running for more than 540 yards.

1919: In 1919, as more than 25 race riots erupted in major U.S. cities, Fritz Pollard, a former Brown University All-American running back, joined the Akron Pros, a pro football team that would later become a charter member of the NFL. "It was evident my first year at Akron back in 1919 that they didn't want Blacks in there getting that money. And here I was playing and coaching and pulling down the **highest salary** in Pro Football," says Fritz Pollard.

1920: Fritz Pollard was the first African American to play professional football with the Akron Pros, In 1920, The team would go on and win the *World Championship* in football.

1920: Fritz Pollard and Bobby Marshall were the first two African American players in the NFL in 1920.

1921: Fritz Pollard achieved one of the greatest honors that any Black man could want. He became the co-head coach of the Akron Pros, while still playing running back for the team that he was coaching.

1922: Fritz Pollard signed a contract with the Milwaukee Badgers. Milwaukee Badgers was a professional American football team, based in Milwaukee, Wisconsin, that played in the National Football League from 1922 to 1926. The Milwaukee team was claimed by the Green Bay Packers and they still reserve two games a season for their old Milwaukee ticket holders, and their radio station as well. He founded the F.D. Pollard and Co. investment firm in 1922.

1923: Fritz Pollard was the first Black quarterback on an NFL team. He was the head coach for the Hammond Pros. Fritz Pollard was inducted into Hammond Pros Hall of Famers in 2005, which inducted George Papa Bear Halas in 1963. The Hammond Pros from Hammond, Indiana played in the National Football League from 1920 to 1926 as a traveling team.

1928: Fritz Pollard established The Chicago Black Hawks (American Football) an all-African-American professional football team. Fritz Pollard was the team's owner, coach, quarterback, and running back. The team played most of its games on the road due to the country's economic situation and poor fan attendance. The team was disbanded three years later in 1932.

1930: Pollard founded his own professional football team, the Brown Bombers.

1935: Fritz Pollard coached an all-Black team in New York (Brown Bombers) from 1935-1938. He also founded the first Black tabloid, the New York Independent News.

1936: Fritz Pollard's son, Fritz Pollard Jr. who played football at the University of North Dakota, was a member of the US Track team at the 1936 Olympics along with Jessie Owens and Ralph Metcalf, who won bronze in the 110 hurdles.

1940: Fritz divorced his first wife, Ada Laing.

1947: Pollard married Mary Ella Austin.

1954: Fritz Pollard was inducted into the National College Hall of Fame.

1956: Fritz Pollard produced Rockin the Blues which included such performers as The Wanderers, The Hurricanes, Elyce Roberts, Linda Hopkins, Pearl Woods, The Five Miller Sisters, The Harptones, and Connie Carroll. Pollard launched the music careers of many African Americans.

1981: Brown University awarded Pollard an honorary doctorate.

1986: Fritz Pollard died of pneumonia, aged 92, on May 11th.

2003: The Fritz Pollard Alliance was founded by a group of National Football League personnel. The focus of the alliance is to open up more opportunities for people of color to coach and administer the game.

2005: Fritz Pollard was inducted into the NFL Hall of Fame in Canton, Ohio.

"They threw rocks at me and called me all kinds of names. But I was there to play football. I had to duck under the rocks and the fellas trying to hurt me."

-Fritz Pollard

Sound Advice from Collegiate Expert Dr. Valencia Belle

Mental Health Deterioration:

Athlete #1

Athlete #1 was drafted in the first round of the NBA. A first-generation college student, Athlete #1 had no other family members to prepare him for the mental, physical, and emotional toll that professional basketball demands.

While earning an average score of 21 out of a possible high score of 36 on the ACT, Athlete #1 secured an athletic scholarship only. His singular focus was to play in the NBA. Therefore, Athlete #1 did the minimal amount of collegiate academic work required to maintain eligibility to play college basketball.

As the years of NBA play took their toll on Athlete #1's mental health, he fell prey to pain medication and sex addiction, fathering 14 children with 10 different women. Due to his inability to graduate from college, despite his extensive knowledge of the game, Athlete #1 could not return to college basketball as a college coach.

In addition, Athlete #1 lacked financial literacy; his accumulated debt meant Athlete #1 owed more money than he could ever repay in this lifetime to agents and creditors. Athlete #1 suffered from depression and subsequently succumbed to a mental breakdown. Due to infidelity, he found himself divorced.

Soon after, Athlete #1 was placed in a treatment facility to detox. After rehabilitation, Athlete #1 attempted to regain his mental and physical strength but found it very difficult to pursue gainful employment measuring up to his pro-career status. With child support challenges and tax liability implications, Athlete #1 was forced to file for bankruptcy.

The moral of this story is that professional athlete status never lasts. It is imperative to earn college degrees from athletic scholarships given to insure lasting financial freedom with sound financial counsel. Lacking these key elements could lead to a mental breakdown.

Arrest & Time Served:

Athlete #2

Athlete #2 was an outstanding college football player drafted to the NFL in the 5th round. Athlete #2 had an outstanding NFL career in front of him. However, Athlete #2 chose to allow his past friends who dealt drugs to sidetrack his future.

Athlete #2 and his entire "crew "of NFL teammates and players were arrested for drug trafficking, which resulted in Athlete #2 being reprimanded by the law and placed in federal prison. Although reared by God-fearing parents who warned Athlete #2 of the dangers of drugs and choosing the wrong friends from the wrong crowd, Athlete #2 failed to listen to wise counsel. After serving his sentence in federal prison, Athlete #2 had a felony record. Earning a felony made it very difficult for Athlete #2 to secure employment. A felony record cannot be expunged. The criminal record remains part of one's permanent record, inhibits access to many things such as pursuing a medical career in hospitals, and limits a person's ability to pursue gainful employment. Athlete #2 even lost his ability to vote. He never was fully restored to the life he would have enjoyed had he made better decisions.

The moral of this story is that professional athletes should evaluate their circle of friends and acquaintances constantly, as well as heed wise counsel.

Rising Above:

Athlete #3

Athlete #3 was a first-generation college student who was unsuccessful 5 times in earning the necessary standardized test score to advance to collegiate play. His parents were forced to raise nearly $40,000 to pay for Athlete #3 to attend a college preparatory school in the hopes it would raise both his standardized test score and his grade point average to earn the right to play college football.

Although Athlete #3 lived in a drug and violence-filled environment, Athlete #3 was raised by his entire "village." His early anger management and fighting problems fueled his football prowess, and Athlete #3 learned to lean on this faith in God to abate his tremendous temper. With proper coaching and guidance, Athlete #3 transitioned successfully to play college and professional football.

Although undrafted, Athlete #3 played 3 seasons in the NFL after becoming the first in his family to graduate from college. He used the knowledge obtained while earning his college degree to align himself with successful business people and used his funds to invest in many lucrative business ventures. He invested his professional earnings into diversified real estate and venture capital ventures, netting huge dividends.

The moral of this story is that professional athletes are not defined by the draft or their length of time playing professional sports. The character of the player determines their success in life while on and off the field.

An International Sensation:

Athlete #4

Athlete #4 was the daughter of a college-educated mother and father who instilled in her early the value of an education. Because her academic and athletic talents were so gifted, Athlete #4 earned her college acceptance with athletic and academic opportunities, completing her college degree with honors.

At the time that Athlete #4 graduated from college, there were not many professional opportunities for women in basketball in the United States. Athlete #4 chose to play basketball internationally, which required her to often travel many miles away from her hometown to foreign countries. Athlete #4 was blessed to have never been involved in any issues with the law, which would have limited her ability to obtain a passport to travel abroad.

Her degree gave her the flexibility of teaching Physical Education in the off-season while she trained for her upcoming foreign basketball seasons.

The moral of this story is that opportunity favors the prepared. Athlete #4 was prepared to play basketball in another country to make her dream become a reality.

—

Student Guidebook:

How to Academically Begin Your College Football Career
by Educational Counselor Dr. Valencia Belle

How Do I Help My Dream of Becoming An NFL Player A Reality?

First, you have to make good grades and play great sports!
It is a two-part process. Academics + Athletics!

Academics (NCAA /Core GPA) and NCAA Clearance

NCAA

There are different divisions, or levels of play and different qualifications for each division.

To be eligible to play at the Division 1 Level, you must qualify through the NCAA.

You will register online at www.ncaa.org.

There is a fee to register that must be paid by debit or credit card.

If you are eligible for free or reduced lunch, the registration fee can be waived by requesting a fee waiver online during NCAA registration.

The NCAA will require you to have a 2.3 Core GPA to earn NCAA clearance at the Division I Level.

Your Core GPA is the GPA used in your 10-7 Qualification Period. This is the GPA average of your top 10 Core grades used to compute your GPA during the Fall Semester of your Senior Year.

During that period, the NCAA will calculate your Core GPA using your highest grades in 10 of your Core classes.

Core Classes are English, Math, History, and Science.

Other core classes are listed on your state's 48-H list.

These other core classes can be substituted, if taken, for core classes with lower grades.

The NCAA will require you to send an official transcript directly to their office.

The NCAA will evaluate your transcript for Core classes completed.

The address is:

NCAA Headquarters
700 W Washington St,
Indianapolis, IN 46204

How Do I Help My Dream of Becoming An NFL Player A Reality?

A student-athlete may be required to take the ACT or SAT to be admitted to college and/or earn academic merit-based scholarships for college.

If you receive free or reduced lunch, you may receive free fee waiver vouchers to take the ACT or SAT for free. Please ask your high school Guidance Counselor for more details about registering for the ACT or SAT with a free fee waiver voucher

ACT

The highest score you can make on the ACT is 36.

You register for the ACT online at www.actstudent.org.

You are allowed to send your score to 4 colleges and universities for free when registering for the ACT.

You should send your ACT score directly to the NCAA as one of your 4 free school codes.

The SCHOOL CODE for the NCAA is 9999.

There is a registration fee for the ACT with or without Writing. The fee for the ACT with Writing costs more. Writing is not required or a part of your ACT composite score.

The ACT Composite score (1-36) is used for college admission.

A 19 ACT Composite will gain admission to many US colleges and universities and may earn athleticism but not academic merit-based scholarships.

The ACT Composite score is an average of the ACT English, Math, Reading, and Science scores.

The ACT will require an ACT 18 English score and an ACT 20 Math score to avoid taking Remedial Classes in college. ACT scores in English or Math that are lower than ACT 18 English and 20 ACT Math will require you to take a placement test, like the TEAS or COMPASS Test, to determine proper class placement.

Remedial Classes are fewer than Freshman level classes that must be passed to earn the right to take Freshman level classes.

Remedial classes must be paid for, but do not count toward graduation or your major.

It is important to research the requirements for admission, academic merit-based scholarships, and eligibility requirements for your college or university of choice.

Academic merit-based, or presidential, scholarships are based on your GPA and/or ACT and SAT scores.

SAT

The highest score you can make on the SAT is 1600.

You register for the SAT online at www.collegeboard.org. You are allowed to send your score to 4 colleges and universities for free when registering for the SAT.

You should send your SAT scores directly to the NCAA as one of your 4 free school codes.

The SCHOOL CODE for the NCAA is 9999.

There is a registration fee for the SAT.

The SAT Composite score (400 - 1600) is used for college admission.

A 1020 SAT Composite will gain admission to many US colleges and universities and may earn athleticism but not academic merit-based scholarships.

The SAT Composite score is an average of the SAT Written Language, Reading, Math with Calculator, and Math without Calculator scores.

Remember, if you are not accepted as a student at the college or university, you cannot be a student-athlete that plays sports for that college or university.

How Do I Help My Dream of Becoming An NFL Player A Reality?

Try to have scored as close to a perfect ACT 36 or SAT 1600 by the end of the Summer before your Senior year, and NCAA 10/7 Qualification, begins.

You can take the ACT 12 times in your lifetime to Superscore. ACT will use the highest score in all 4 areas to Superscore.

You can take the SAT an unlimited number of times in your lifetime to Superscore. SAT will use the highest score in all 4 areas to Superscore.

You should begin taking the ACT or SAT as early as possible. You can register online at age 13.

It is to your advantage to take the ACT all 12 times, or the SAT as many times as you need to score as close to an ACT 36 or SAT 1600 perfect score as possible.

All colleges and universities accept both the ACT and SAT scores.

You should take an ACT or SAT prep course to prepare for the ACT or SAT before taking the actual standardized test.

If you need help with ACT or SAT prep, calculating your Core GPA, or NCAA Clearance guidance, contact:

Dr. Valencia Belle
ACT Certified Educator
SCHOOLS /CLEARED Programs
www.schoolsprograms.org
schoolsprograms@gmail.com
Text your questions to (251) 298-7111

Who is Gary Burley?

A young Gary Burley

Former American football player **Gary Steven Burley** was a Defensive End and a part of the first American Football Conference (AFC) Championship in Cincinnati Bengals history who went through incredible trials and tribulations. He played nine seasons for the Bengals before playing the final season of his career for the Atlanta Falcons in the National Football League.

Gary is the 5-year-old wearing a gray jacket

"G.B." as he was known, was a member of the franchise's first Super Bowl appearance during the 1981-82 season. In his career, G.B. played in 105 games for the Bengals. The 6 foot 3-inch tall imposing player accrued four fumble returns, two sacks, and a safety. Gary Steven Burley is an alumnus of The University of Pittsburgh, Grove City High School, and Brookpark Middle School, Grove City, Ohio, a suburb of Columbus.

An artist (Hollis Strunk) created this statuette for Burley. The realistic representation shows the orange and black uniform Burley wore.

After his NFL career had ended, the football veteran founded a non-profit organization where he resides in Birmingham, Alabama. Called *Pro Start Academy*, P.S.A. is an organization of retired NFL Players which mentors young athletes. On its website, it says," *We want to give student-athletes a competitive advantage by building a bridge to success on and off the field of play.*"

Gary Burley runs non-profit Pro Start Academy, a
sports and academic academy for kids

Pro Start Academy brings in top business executives to teach kids how they can ascend from the loading dock to the board room. Burley has done much fund-raising and work for gifted middle and high school athletes. Burley continues this day to mentor the most talented and intelligent young athletes all across the United States.

The former defensive lineman's love of football is clear but his love of giving back is what motivates him. The father of four children and grandfather to 12 grandchildren is passionate about helping young people achieve their dreams of making it in the Pros.

Gary fought off life-threatening ailments including cancer, a bone marrow transplant, and a bout of salmonella poisoning that put him in a wheelchair for six months.

Gary spent the next three years—four hours a day, three days a week—undergoing dialysis and hoping for a life-saving kidney donation. If that wasn't enough, following years of dialysis dependency, he needed surgery for a kidney transplant. He also suffered a stroke and needed brain surgery for a stroke. He underwent a left-hip replacement and gall bladder replacement, appendectomy, making him a bionic man.

Gary and Bobbie with some of his 12 grandchildren

Humbled and grateful to be alive, Gary delights in aiding young people in their journey to the NFL. Gary hopes to give the next generation assistance and guidance. He says he wants to return the favor given to him long ago when two men believed in him. He feels that is why his life was spared.

"I took Chemo for a year in 2014. It didn't get any better or worse so Dr. Lorena Adrijana de Idiaquez Bakula of the University of Alabama of Birmingham said it was time for a bone marrow transplant. Those words still haunt me today. You have a thousand thoughts going through your head at one time." The procedure was painful and it would take weeks to recover from it. Gary had to make a decision.

"Well, my first worry of finding a donor was put to rest when I found out I could use my own stem cells so now we can move forward with the transplant. I spent three months in the hospital. I was finally released and home for a week when I was sent back to the hospital for another month. It seems that I contracted a virus in the hospital. I was laying in bed surrounded by a room full of doctors. I noticed they all had the same grim look on their faces and it wasn't good.

"I heard one of the doctors say, 'He's not going to make it. The virus is spreading and it's in his kidney. If it moves to his heart, it's all over.'"

Gary fell asleep, exhausted and dejected. He had tackled fast-moving and quick players on the field. But he couldn't tackle and tame this diagnosis.

Gary's Grandmother, Juanita Abbott, Mom Mary Burley,
Dad Ray Burley, Cousin Reggie Ivory (Left to right)

Ray Burley, Gary's father

Gary's mother, Mary Burley

"My mother and father came to visit me in the hospital room. My Mom was rubbing my head like she did when I was a little boy and my Father was in the restroom reading the newspaper."

"Mom leans over gently and in a soft comforting voice tells me, "Peace Be Still," which was the title of a Reverend James Cleveland Gospel Song from 1963 that we listened to every Sunday before Church."

I could hear the lyrics in my mind. The music dominated my thoughts. The song went like this: *"I don't want to be afraid every time I face the waves. I don't want to fear the storm."* Gary recalled his mother's sweet voice as she rubbed Gary's forehead gently. *"Peace be still"* she whispered. Gary's mind floated to that song's melody, something he remembers hearing from childhood to adulthood. He reflected on that quiet, peaceful moment, remembering more lyrics, "You are here so it is well, Even when my eyes can't see I will trust the voice that speaks."

"Then Dad said, "That's Right.""

"When I woke up my wife was working at the foot of my bed.

"I said, 'Honey, where's my Mom? I can smell her perfume.'

"Bobbie looked at me like I was crazy.

"Then she said these words: 'Honey, your Mom has been in heaven for 25 years.'"

"I knew then and there that God had a plan for me. My doctors came in soon after and told me that there are no signs of the deadly virus. That's when I thanked God and told him I would do anything. I can pay it forward and thank him for allowing me to be with my wife and kids and grandkids."

Gary's arduous journey was far from over.

"I was healthy and happy when I got a call from my doctor who wanted to check my kidneys. They found out I had more health issues as a result of years of high blood pressure and chemotherapy. I'd damaged my kidneys to the point where I needed to go on dialysis for three and a half years."

Gary wrote about the need to accelerate the process in the *Birmingham Times* in 2020, "I waited for three years, patiently attending dialysis appointments, until I finally got my match. I'm one of the lucky ones. Right now in our country, kidney disease impacts 37 million people, and for the nearly three-quarters of a million people who require a kidney transplant, they have to get in line behind 100,000 other Americans already on the waiting list.

One of the many things I learned playing in the NFL was then when you take a hit, you get back up and play the next down. Despite the hits I took when I battled cancer and received my kidney transplant, I was able to get back up through the help of excellent doctors and health professionals. I owe it to them and to everyone still on that transplant waitlist to continue fighting for the necessary treatment solutions. I hope Congress will hear the call to fund and support KidneyX, and spur what could be one of the most ambitious medical breakthroughs of our time. Dialysis treatment, the only other therapy available for people with kidney failure, saves lives and is no doubt a necessary piece in treating people with kidney disease. However, nearly 60 percent of people who start hemodialysis today will die within five years. I was raised to believe that in America, we could be anything or do anything we wanted, and I think this ideal still holds true even for tough medical challenges."

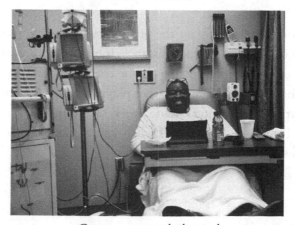

Gary recovers in the hospital

Gary didn't give up. Instead, he looked up.

"I prayed and asked for a kidney donor. Fifty-five people who offered were not matches. Then God sent my old friend Jarralynne Agee & Dr. Bob Agee. Lo, and behold Jarralynne was a perfect blood and tissue match. I've been the lucky recipient of God's blessings. To me, that means I have no other choice but to pay it forward."

Jarralynne Agee, who gave Gary her kidney reflected back, saying she felt responsible for him in a custodial way. "I knew a social media post asking for a kidney, was talking to me. I definitely think it was a spiritual touch that I got that let me know this was what I was supposed to do."

She says her husband and family supported her decision. "I really appreciate Gary." Jarralynne broke down into tears, getting emotional. "It's one of the things (giving Gary her kidney) I feel the most good about in my **entire** life. So when I see him doing stuff, I'm proud even though he was grateful, I was very proud. I guess he's my big brother and Bobbie is my big sister."

Since his recovery, the once strong force of nature on the football field has become a fierce advocate for cancer research, kidney transplant, and youth development through proceeds from his annual celebrity golf tournament. Burley hopes proceeds from the book will aid him to continue to pay it forward.

Football Aspirations

Gary Burley's dream about the possibility of playing football started when he was in high school when his uncle Johnny Boy (known as JB) took him to the very first professional game he ever attended. He recalls being 16 or 17. The Cleveland Browns were playing that day. The Minnesota Vikings Purple People Eaters made every tackle in the first half of the game. That impressed him. That's when young Gary decided he wanted to play professional football.

Johnny Boy Ivory (known as JB), Gary's Uncle
JB took Gary to his first professional football game

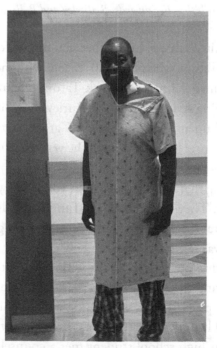

Gary Burley walks the halls following one of many surgeries
at the University of Alabama Hospital

1976, 1977 and 1978. Gary Burley was part of the one of the greatest Bengals defensive lines nicknamed "The WEBB Defense" - W-Whitley, E-Edwards, B-Burley and B-Browner

As a non-recruited athlete, his mother sent him to football camp where he met safety Jack Tatum, who played 10 seasons with the Oakland Raiders, and offensive lineman John Hicks. Jack Tatum, nicknamed *The Assassin* because of his playing style, asked where Burley was going to college. Gary said he would end up at "Westinghouse." Gary meant Westinghouse the appliance manufacturer but Jack thought he was referring to Westinghouse College Prep School.

Despite hearing that naive answer from young Gary, the pair took him under their wings. They taught him the fundamentals of the sport, gave advice on how to take the college entrance exam, and gave the wannabe a glimpse of what was needed to get into college.

"I was allowed to not only workout with them but to be mentored by them before entering the NFL Draft. I learned so much from them that at that moment I promised myself, 'One day, I'm going to do the same thing for kids and help them achieve success on and off the field of play.'"

The ambitious high school student met a counselor from Columbus East high school who approached Gary and guided him through the process. After weighing his options, Gary chose to go to Junior College and then seek to transfer to a 4-year college or university.

Gary had been accepted to Wharton County Junior College in Wharton, Texas, far away from his hometown in Urbancrest, Ohio.

"I had never been on an airplane before," he recalled.

The frightened young athlete flew to Texas; he was "scared to death." He remembers feeling lost. "I didn't know what was going on."

Arriving in the Lone Star state, Gary remembered the training that Jack and John taught him. Gary recalls that the professional football players knew what he needed to learn and what he should expect; Gary followed his mentors' instruction and advice, allowing himself to be coached and as a result, believes he "got lucky."

He soon showed himself to be an outstanding athlete and became an "All-American".

Besides luck, there was hard work and talent involved. Gary did what some athletes could only dream about. Proudly clad in white pants, a Black jersey, and wearing a protective orange helmet, Burley participated in the most notable game in Bengals history known for the coldest temperature in NFL history in terms of wind chill.

G.B. recalls playing in the "Freezer Bowl." He remembers that it felt like it was 30 below when the Bengals played in the AFC Championship game against the San Diego Chargers. The Bengals defeated the Chargers 27-7. It was one of the few games in NFL history in which the same team kicked off to begin both halves. Cincinnati won the toss. Instead of receiving, Cincinnati chose to have the brutally cold wind at their backs to start the game. San Diego, trailing 17-7 at halftime, exercised its option at the beginning of the second half to receive the kickoff. That resulted in Cincinnati kicking off to begin both halves and in the same direction both times.

Gary's fondest memory happened when the game ended and Gary looked up from the field. In the stands, despite the bone-chillingly frigid temperatures, he saw four shirtless fans, then heard the announcers' booming voice bellowing out that the Bengals were headed to the Super Bowl! What a sweet sound that was! His hard work had paid off.

Along with his teammates, Gary was headed to the Pontiac Silver Dome in Pontiac, Michigan for **Super Bowl XVI**. On January 24th,

1982, the Bengals faced the San Francisco 49ers, who prevailed 26-21 in a game played in front of 85 million fans. It was one of the most watched broadcasts in American television history.

At the start of the Super Bowl, the boy from a small town in Ohio remembers standing on the sideline next to Diana Ross just before she sang *The Star Spangled Banner*. Diana asked the fans in the stands if they "could sing with authority" and asked those under the enclosed dome to sing with her. You could hear the voices of fans chime in as Diana Ross belted out the anthem, articulating each word. Burley remembers feeling a sense of accomplishment, knowing, "that we reached a pinnacle that some teams never reach."

Burley appreciates the moment and savors it until this day. "I'm here with a memory that will last forever and that no one can take away."

Clearing the Air

Time can heal. Gary recalls going to play the Minnesota Vikings and Fran Tarkenton's story "was killing us. We couldn't get near him and then I broke free and sacked him. I got up but he was still on the ground. I had broken his leg. It was a clean hit but I had to have a police escort out of the Stadium."

"25 years later I went to an event where he (Fran Tarkenton) was the guest speaker and when he saw me in the audience he called me up on stage and re-enacted the whole game. In the end, he vindicated me by saying it was a clean hit."

Burley also recalls working hard at practice, doing his best to be on time and work hard, but he didn't always succeed.

"I remember Forrest Gregg who coached the Bengals to their first Super Bowl. Coach Gregg made me pee my pants when he yelled at me in front of the whole team, " Gary recalled.

"We usually practiced at 3:00. I left to go to lunch at 1:00 pm. At 1:30 he moved practice back an hour. When I got back the whole team was on the field. When I drove up I almost passed out. I was panicking and sweating. I had to run inside and get dressed in my uniform and get back on the field with everybody else.

Well, I did and thought I dodged that bullet. Boy! Was I wrong! I got down to start stretching. As soon as I did this 6' 1, 270 lb. ex-NFL terror started Blessing me out in front of the whole team. I still have nightmares about that!

Stay Away From Joe Namath

Burley played against and amongst the best of them, including Joe Namath. Namath was the first quarterback to win both a college national championship and a major professional championship.

Gary recalls how stunned he was the first time he faced off against Joe Namath:

"When I was a Rookie we played the New York Jets. When we were warming up before the game All-Pro Offensive Lineman Winston Hill came up to me and said he'd heard about my reputation for getting to the Quarterback."

Then Winston Hill turned and pointed to Joe Namath and said, "'You won't get near that guy who pays for my house and kids. You won't get near him." I turned to walk away and I saw my feet in the air. He picked me up and slammed me in the mud. I was on the ground trying to wipe all the mud off my face. I had the opportunity to tell Joe that story last year at ProStart Academy's Celebrity Golf Tournament.

Recruited

The young college student was on a recruiting trip after attending two years of school in Wharton, Texas when he overheard Coach Jackie Sherill of Iowa State say:

"If they could get the Burley kid out of Texas, the team could have a winning year."

The players were gathered in a steam room, sitting around, wrapped in towels, hidden by steam, when Jackie Sherill looked around to see if he could recruit promising players.

After the condensation in the steam room began to clear, Coach Sherill approached him. "Do you know the Burley kid?"

Gary strung the coach along for a bit at first, laughing to himself. Coach asked Gary Burley if he could get him an introduction to Gary Burley! Gary could hardly contain himself. He decided to play along. Yes, he knew Gary Burley. And yes, he knew him well enough to talk to him. "I can get you an introduction," promised Gary, amused and knowing he could make good on the promise. When he couldn't continue the ruse any longer, Gary revealed to Coach Sherill that he was talking to Gary Burley. He told the coach he wanted to live closer to home. He applied to the University of Pittsburgh, which wasn't far from where he grew up. Burley redirected his studies on and off the field, accepting a scholarship where he was named an All-American.

All-American

The 6-foot-3, 274-pound rusher was honored when named an All-American in 1973-74 at the University of Pittsburgh. The title is given to outstanding U.S. athletes.

Bobbie Knight Burley (left) and Gary Burley (right).

Burley's football card

*Gary Burley (left), Ken Riley II (middle), NFL Hall of Famer
Ken Riley (right) at 50-year Bengals reunion*

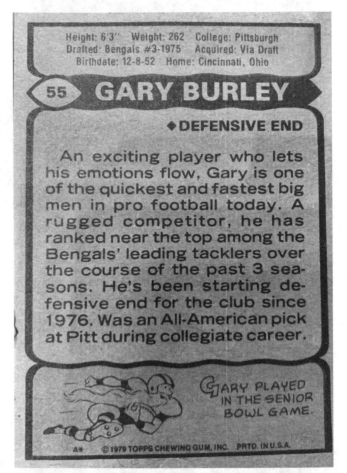

Height: 6'3" Weight: 262 College: Pittsburgh
Drafted: Bengals #3-1975 Acquired: Via Draft
Birthdate: 12-8-52 Home: Cincinnati, Ohio

55 GARY BURLEY

◆DEFENSIVE END

An exciting player who lets his emotions flow, Gary is one of the quickest and fastest big men in pro football today. A rugged competitor, he has ranked near the top among the Bengals' leading tacklers over the course of the past 3 seasons. He's been starting defensive end for the club since 1976. Was an All-American pick at Pitt during collegiate career.

GARY PLAYED IN THE SENIOR BOWL GAME.

A✶ © 1979 TOPPS CHEWING GUM, INC. PRTD. IN U.S.A.

Height 6'3" Weight 262 College: Pittsburgh Drafted: Bengals #3-1975 Acquired Via Draft Birthdate: 12-8-52 Home: Cincinnati, Ohio 55 Gary Burley Defensive End. "An exciting player who lets his emotions flow, Gary is one of the quickest and fastest big men in pro football today. A rugged competitor, he has ranked near the top among the Bengals' leading tacklers over the course of the past 3 seasons. He's been starting defensive end for the club since 1976. Was an All-American pick at Pitt during their collegiate career. Gary played in the Senior Bowl Game."

Share

Gary Burley celebrates a win against the San Diego Chargers in 1981.
Photo used with permission by the Associated Press

Pro Start kids attend camp

Gary and some of his grandkids

Philadelphia Eagles Quarterback Jalen Hurts (left) poses with
Bobbie Knight Burley (center) and Gary Burley (right)

Gary Burley was honored by his alma mater, Grove City High School for playing part of Super Bowl History. He gave the school a gold-painted football and his old cleats

Birmingham Mayor Randall Woodfin congratulates Gary Burley
(Wikipedia)

In 1977, Bengals Defensive End Gary Burley '67 faces
Earl Campbell of the Houston Oilers
(on right, facing Gary)

2016-Burley gives money to Grove City High School, his alma mater

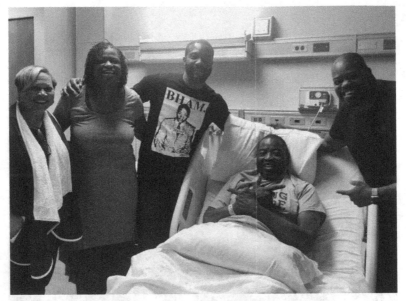

Wife Bobby (left to right), Kidney Donor Jarralynne Agee,
Birmingham Mayor Randall Woodfin, Kidney Recipient Gary Burley and
Dr. Robert Agee in UAB Hospital following the transplant

Gary Burley (left) hugs Joe Namath (middle)
and Coach Jackie Sherill (right) at Greystone Golf & Country Club

When Burley played at University of Pittsburgh, a cartoon was created showing how Georgia Tech players feared Burley's fierceness

No. 67, 73

Position: Defensive end

Personal information

Born: December 8, 1952 (age 69)
Urbancrest, Ohio
Height: 6 ft 3 in (1.91 m)
Weight: 272 lb (123 kg)

Career information

High school: Grove City
(Grove City, Ohio)

College: Pittsburgh
NFL Draft: 1976 / Round: 3 / Pick: 55

Career history

- Cincinnati Bengals (1976–1983)
- Atlanta Falcons (1984)

Career highlights and awards

- PFWA All-Rookie Team (1976)

Career NFL statistics

Sacks: 37.0

Safeties: 1

Source credit: Wikipedia
Burley is chasing San Diego Chargers' Quarterback Dan Fouts

Who is Co-Author Ralph Brooks?

Ralph V. Brooks is a sports and children's book author and advocate for advancing childhood literacy. He is from Eufaula, Alabama. He is the son of hard-working and determined parents, Mary and Ralph Brooks, Sr. His parents had a limited education. His father didn't get past the third grade. His mother graduated after eighth grade. Ralph, Jr. was the first in his family to go to college. Ralph desired to achieve more than his parents by furthering his education.

As an elementary student, Ralph Jr. was very eager and committed to learning the fundamentals of reading. When he was in the fourth grade, Mrs. Emma S. Mask, Ralph's English teacher, noticed a spark in his eyes as he embraced the desire to learn to read. At the time, he was struggling and falling behind his classmates who were learning to read and comprehend their assignments on a more advanced level.

Brooks recalls, "I was often afraid to pronounce certain words and felt embarrassed that I could not seek help from those nearest to me." His motivation grew from his inability to read in 1972 to being a notable author who has published six books to date. In 2004, Brooks wrote his first book, *"Day by Day Living with Epilepsy "* as a self-help guide to educate individuals about seizures. He was inspired to write the book because his father would have a "seizure and we would try to put a spoon or wallet in his mouth. It was the wrong thing to do. The paramedics would even bring a plastic tube. No one knew what to do in the 70s and 80s."

In 2006, Brooks took pen to paper again when he wrote *"89 - the Road to Number One"* a memoir about how Brooks played high school sports and participated in the 1981 Football State Championship team his junior year in Eufaula, Alabama. During his senior year, he moved back to Jackson Gap, Alabama where he spent most of his childhood days. He then led the high school Dadeville Tigers in Dadeville, Alabama to another Football State Championship game. The team had won the Football State championship in 1981, the same year as he did in Eufaula, Alabama. Says Brooks, "I was lost for words when Legendary Auburn Head Football Coach, Pat Dye, came into the locker room and invited me to attend an Auburn game before the Football State Championship game." Brooks was inspired after watching the Auburn game and meeting the entire team.

Brooks played in the Football State Championship game the next week in Dadeville, Alabama. His team lost to the visiting Hazelwood Bears of Town Creek, Alabama by a score of 29-16.

Brooks played against his good friend, Kerry Goode, a former running back for the University of Alabama who became a professional American Football player. He played four seasons for the Tampa Bay Buccaneers and Miami Dolphins.

Brooks tragically suffered a severe neck injury in the last play of the State Championship game. That injury abruptly ended his promising career. He never got a chance to fulfill his dream of playing college football due to having grand mal seizures as a result of his neck injury. The doctor he consulted warned that if he continued to play he would risk losing his life. Brooks made the difficult decision to end his football career but channeled his passion for the sport in other ways.

Between 2018-2019 Ralph Brooks wrote and published four children's books, two of them written in both English and Spanish. He was inspired after reading the book, *"The Secret"* by Rhonda Byrne. He loved the book so much that he read it nine times. One of his children's books titled, *"Three Words"* was dedicated to the Philippines to show appreciation for the abundance of love given to him and his best friend, Darrell Ingram, Vice President of "BrooksandBooks", during their travels that started in 2009 and continues today.

According to a 2011 report by the Annie E. Casey Foundation, "A first grader who reads below grade level is at a marked disadvantage, and teachers might have to spend additional time helping the child catch up. Children who don't read at grade level by third grade are four times more likely to drop out of high school." This being said, Brooks believes his books are one added value to help the fight against illiteracy and break the barrier of children reading below their grade levels." Brooks' books are available on Amazon.com.

*Dr. Valencia Belle (left), Gary Burley (middle) and Ralph Brooks (right)
hanging out at the Celebrity Golf tournament in Birmingham, Alabama.*

Brooks' Accomplishments:

1980 - Awarded A.M.M.S. (Admiral Moore Middle School) Outstanding running back in Eufaula, Alabama at the team football banquet. Brooks played so well as a freshman that the Head football coach of the Eufaula High School moved him up as a ninth grader to play with the varsity Football Team.

1981 - Eufaula Tigers win the 3A Football State Championship game on December 8, in Hartselle, Alabama. Brooks was a part of this team in his junior year. He received his high school championship ring in 1982.

1982 - Brooks moved from Eufaula, Alabama to Jackson Gap, Alabama to play for the Dadeville Tigers. He led the defending State Championship back to the big dance. The team came up a little short and lost the game 29-16 to the Hazelwood Bears in Dadeville, Alabama. His team finished the 1982 season as 2A Football State Runners-up.

1983 - Brooks' senior year. He received the "100% Award " for outstanding all-around player on offense, defense, and specialty teams. Brooks was the first recipient in the school's history to have received this award. The coaches voted to grant this award because of Brooks' love for the game, dedication, leadership in the locker room, and positive attitude toward each game. Brooks graduated in May 1983, from Dadeville High School in Dadeville, Alabama.

1986 - Brooks moved to Tampa, Florida, and attended Tampa College. He received his six-month certificate in Introduction to Computers and made the Dean's list four times out of the six months in the program.

1991- Brooks participated in his First Great American Teach-In at Chamberlain High School in Tampa, Florida. He spoke to the students about thinking outside of the box and being different.

1995 - Brooks received the Sallie Mae Award (Community Service Man of the Year) for four years of service in Hillsborough County's youth reading program. Sallie Mae donated $1000 in Ralph Brooks' name to Pearson Elementary School, which was presented to him by the Sallie Mae organization.

1997 - Brooks became Flag Football Head Coach for the boys, ages seven to nine, at the YMCA in Tampa, Florida. In his first year as coach, his team won the championship. At the end of the season, he received the "Bronze Level Award" for mentoring youth during their practice time on the field.

2000 - Brooks received the "Editor's Choice Award " from the Montel Williams Cure for MS Poetry Contest.

2001 - Brooks won the JP Morgan Chase "Employee of the Month Award " a recognition he won three times within the same year and also received $700 each month. Also, he won the "All-Star Award " and a check for $1,000 and round-trip transportation to New York for the all-star banquet to compete for $5000 amongst the other winners. Brooks' commitment to his community service work earned him the JP Morgan Chase "Profile in Diversity Award " another check for $1,000 and his postcards for diversity.

2004 - Brooks was named Head Baseball Coach for the Wellswood Pony League in Tampa, Florida. His team, Brook's Shetland Ponies, won the Baseball Championship in his first year as Head Coach. On September

17, Brooks had his first book signing at Barnes and Noble (Carrollwood) in Tampa, Florida, for his first published book, "Day by Day Living with Epilepsy".

2005 - Brooks received an "Appreciation Award" from the Admiral Moore Middle School Principal for his $500 donation to the basketball program. He was a two-sport athlete at the school playing both basketball and football for A.M.M S. In addition, he received the "Thank You Award " from Head Soccer Coach Nicole Lehart for his $1,000 donation and sponsorship to Wellswood Tampa Park & Recreation Soccer League. His team, under the leadership of Lehart, finished a perfect season with a perfect 11-0 record to win the Soccer League's Championship. Also, Brooks joins the Tampa City Youth Mentoring and Reading program called "The Serve Volunteers in Education" to volunteer and work more than 200 hours to help contribute to the student's learning abilities. He received recognition from "The President's Volunteer Service Award," signed by George Bush for his involvement with Pop Warner youth football. He coached for 10 years from 2000 until 2010 for the team's "East Tampa Bay Bandits" and Brandon Cowboys where he was voted as Director of Football for the league.

2006 - Brooks published his second book, *#89 The Road to Number One,* and three more children's books beginning in 2018 through 2019, which include Libro Infantl (English and Spanish Edition) Volume 1, Children's Book: Libro Infantl, Volume 2, and Children's Book-Three Words " Don't Ever Quit ". 2019-Children Book: Libro Infantl, Volume 2, and Children Book-Three Words " Don't Ever Quit ".

2009 - Brooks was named one of Humana's Top Supervisors and earned a round-trip first-class ticket to travel to the Philippines. There for 19 days, he assisted and helped train employees in the Customer Service, Billing, and Claims Departments.

2015 - Brooks was recognized by John Brown, the Humana Segment Vice President of Retail Service Operations as the "Medicare Service Operations Person of Character Award" as an exemplary employee who puts people first and focuses on helping others. He was on 14 "Shining Star Awards" from 2006 until 2020 during his 15 years of service with Humana and is still going strong in 2021.

Ralph Brooks (left) and Darrell Ingram (right) host a book signing in Tampa, Florida to promote their Brooks and Book company – "Fight Against Illiteracy".

Meet Co-Author, Editor, and Former CBS Journalist

Donna Francavilla

Lured by the noisy pandemonium of the newsroom, the nail-biting contest of sporting events, the excitement of breaking news, and the desire to describe history as it unfolds, I fell in love with story-telling.

As the daughter of Italian immigrants, I recall witnessing discrimination against non-whites. During the 1960s, Italians were called the "N" word because some were born with dark skin and curly hair. Since I personally saw racial injustice growing up, I welcomed the idea of writing about the brave men who faced discrimination head-on and overcame it.

Both my parents arrived on American shores as young adults who didn't know a word of English. They met in Philadelphia a couple of years later, taking English classes and proudly becoming American citizens. My parents told me that 4 young men originally from Italy were walking on Broad Street when spotted 4 young women also from Italy. That chance meeting resulted in 3 life-long marriages! Aurora married Lelio Ciccotelli and bore four children (two doctors, one lawyer, and a journalist).

My generation was the first to attend not only college and graduate school but high school since our mother was not educated past 5th grade.

Like the men we write about who were the first to make sacrifices in football, my parents faced adversity. My maternal grandmother Raffaella DeVuono was among the 600,000 victims in impoverished Southern Italy who contracted and died from the Spanish Flu (influenza) in a pandemic that claimed the lives of 21 million around the globe. My maternal grandmother Raffaella passed away in front of my 5-year-old frightened mother, Aurora DeVuono. Due to political strife, Aurora's father fled Italy for Buenos Aires. Aurora was left without parents, feeling abandoned and alone. Before she died, Raffaella had the foresight to arrange to send her daughter to an orphanage run by nuns. Under the care of the nuns, Aurora prayed every day for 20 years. She asked God to live in America with the only family she had left.

Aurora's grandmother, Carolina Lanza, answered that prayer. Carolina sent her son to an Embassy to expedite the process. Finally, in 1950, at age 28, a sea-sick Aurora wearing her school uniform and carrying all her possessions in a small bag, arrived from Italy after 3 weeks. The slow boat sailed past the Statue of Liberty in New York City. Aurora was processed through the system on Ellis Island along with many other immigrants, gliding into her new life in America.

Aurora is pictured below as she celebrates her 100th birthday in June of 2022. Mrs. Ciccotelli recalls being alive when the football pioneers we write about in this book were first breaking barriers. She knows first-hand about overcoming challenges like discrimination, poverty, and the strife of world wars.

*100-year-old Italian immigrant Aurora Ciccotelli (above) celebrates
her 100th birthday. Donna's mother poses in front of glamour
shots taken in 1950 when Aurora first came to America.*

Journalism

My career in journalism began innocently enough. During a Rutgers
University public speaking class where we demonstrated the use of props,
I pointed my toes, illustrating ballet moves before Professor Frank Hall.
The former KYW-TV anchor and personality summoned me to him. Mr.
Hall said, "Young lady, have you ever thought about a career in media?"
Frank Hall introduced me to the news director at KYW Newsradio in
Philadelphia, who hired me.

Reporters dubbed me the little fish that out-maneuvered the big fish
in this David v.s. Goliath true tale. In the 1980s, I interviewed Donald
Trump at a press conference, turning the tables on the personable self-
promoter. Trump endorsed the radio station I programmed. Trump told
me, "Hi, I'm Donald Trump and when I'm in Washington, I listen to
WPGC-AM, Business Radio 1580." The story ran in the *Washington Post
and Washington Times.*

In 1990, I moved briefly to Miami where I anchored newscasts part-
time for WINZ-AM Newsradio.

Over the years, I was privileged to cover major stories making news around the American South for CBS Radio, CBS-TV, CBSN, and wire service Agence France Press. I wrote and broadcast about storms such as Hurricane Katrina, reported on major trials, described civil rights marches, interviewed newsmakers, and took a closer look at pivotal elections. I informed CBS news listeners about the major developing news stories in Alabama, Mississippi, and the Florida Panhandle.

I described the controversy surrounding Alabama Judicial Building in Montgomery when then-Alabama Chief Justice Roy Moore secretly ushered into the building during the cover of night, a 10-commandments granite monument. I listened carefully to the dramatic courtroom testimony during the historic 16th Street Baptist Church bombing trials in the early 2000s. Those trials sought to address systematic racism in the judicial system in the United States and after 40 years serve justice on two White men accused in the 1963 bombings of four Black girls.

You can hear a sampling of those stories on Soundcloud:
https://soundcloud.com/donnafrancavilla

My interests extended beyond the South to similar social and cultural conflicts in Europe. In 2000 and 2006, I learned more about the ill and long-lasting effects of another kind of racism, Nazi racism, and the Holocaust. I participated twice in German-American Journalist Exchange Programs called RIAS. While a RIAS Fellow, I studied the divisive effects of racism and discrimination in Europe. Fellows examined German media, politics, and society. We absorbed what we saw and learned there. When I returned home, I produced a 7-part TV series on Alabama's connection to Germany which aired on WVTM-TV and Alabama Public Television.

In my career, I've learned about the devastating consequences of war and conflict and the security of peace and understanding. Attending summits like the G-8 in Bonn, meeting with NATO representatives, and interviewing politicians at the European Union headquarters lent itself to greater understanding. Closer to home, I met and listened to the Dalai Lama when he sat with Birmingham journalists.

Curious about communism, I examined the political environments in communist nations including Poland and Cuba, interviewing Cubans for the *Voice of America* on the 50th anniversary of the Cuban Revolution. Sometimes the reporter becomes part of the story. That was the situation in 2010 when I embarked on a mother-daughter trip in advance of my daughter's wedding. Dangerous mudslides and landslides made bridges and roads impassable at Peru's 15th-century Inca citadel, Machu Picchu. While in the middle of a natural disaster, I waited for 3 hours in line to use the phone on the town's one landline. I called the CBS radio studio in New York, breaking the story, and wrote about it for the RTDNA (Radio and Television Digital News Association). I experienced stress, fear, and adrenaline that accompanied concern for my daughter's safety.

In Peru, I was faced with anti-American sentiment. Americans were abhorred for their perceived power, influence, and financial strength. Many were attacked on the streets of Aguas Calientes while awaiting rescue. After four harrowing days, my daughter Lisa and I were among stranded tourists airlifted to safety by the Peruvian military with the help of the American State Department. I feel the experience helped prepare me to write about the struggles faced by these five great men.

Donna Francavilla (left) and National Talk Show Host Jim Bohonnon

National

Despite the harrowing experience in Peru, I mostly focused on the domestic front, contributing to radio shows including *CBS Radio's World Roundup, and Westwood One's America in the Morning* hosted by the legendary broadcaster Jim Bohonnon, and producing television segments on *CBS TV's Evening News, The Early Show*, and *Oprah's Where Are They Now?* programs. I also wrote news articles for various national and international publications.

I was inspired by some great reporters and anchors whom I was exposed to when serving as an Edward R. Murrow judge for the Radio Television News Directors Association (RTNDA)/Radio Television Digital News Association/RTDNA). Elected Director-at-Large for the RTDNA in 2006, I was able to meet with FCC officials and get a better understanding of the broadcast world. I was later honored to have been included in *Who's Who in the South and Southwest, Who's Who in America,* and *Who's Who in the World* publications.

Local

Also worth mentioning is that I was privileged enough to fill-in as a television reporter at Birmingham television stations WVTM-TV and WBMA-TV. I had fun serving as a talk show host on WAPI-AM/FM as well as hosting a weekly radio show for the Alabama Radio Network which was heard in four markets. The show was called *Frankly Speaking - What women talk about when men aren't around.* It amuses me that the show attracted more curious male listeners than female listeners.

I went on to start a boutique public relations agency, called Frankly Speaking Communications, LLC. I was able to use my voice to describe fairways on *Greystone Golf & Country Club* and promote entities in radio commercials and corporate voice-over projects. Always willing to try new things, this is my first official foray into book publishing.

Ms. Senior Hoover 23 Donna Francavilla

2023 Ms. Senior Hoover Donna Francavilla represents Hoover, where she has lived for nearly 30 years

I had previously edited several other books including Las Vegas talk show host Heidi Harris's 2018 *Don't Pat Me On The Head; Blowback, setbacks, and Comebacks in Vegas Radio,* and worked on first-time author Bill J.W Thomas's 2023 book entitled *Ben's Many Classrooms.*

Achievements

I am a mother of four kind and accomplished children and a grandmother of 5.

While I consider raising my children into productive, caring, compassionate people an achievement, a few other milestones are notable. In 2012, *Shelby Living Magazine* listed me as one of 100 people in the County you need to know. In 2015 I was named *Positive Maturity's Top 50 Over 50* and in 2016, I represented the state as *Alabama Media Professionals' 2016 Communicator of Achievement* for *the National Federation of Press Women.*

Like Gary Burley, I believe in investing in future generations and have contributed time and money toward that mission. A former *President of Alabama Media Professionals,* I currently serve as a volunteer as the non-profit's *Education and Scholarship Chair. The AMP Education Fund* raises awareness for media literacy and raises funds for adult education as well as high school and college scholarships. Some proceeds from this book will benefit the non-profit.

Both co-authors rejoice after both recovered from brain surgeries within 6 months of one-another's. Donna Francavilla (left) and Gary Burley (right) in Hoover, Alabama

I received a thorough education about my community as a graduate of *Leadership Hoover, Leadership Shelby County,* and *Leadership Birmingham.* I enjoyed it so much, I served for 3 terms on the Board of Directors of *Leadership Shelby County.*

Since nuns saved my mother's life and I attended 12 years of Catholic School, I pay it forward by dedicating Sundays to reading scripture at *Saint Mark the Evangelist Catholic Church.* I volunteered on the Italian Food Festival Committee and for 5 years helped market its annual Italian Food Festival.

AMP Education Fund Chairman Donna Francavilla raises scholarship funds for high school and college students

In 2023, officially over the age of 60, I was selected as *Ms. Senior Hoover, Alabama.*

I feel spiritually led to writing this narrative with Gary and Ralph in the hopes that you will find hope and inspiration within its pages.

Destiny

My involvement in the sports community has deeply impacted me. In 1979, together with another dancer, I won the New Jersey state contest for Jazz Dancing. With my schoolmates, I danced on local Philadelphia-area dance programs. Empowered, I minored in dance at Rutgers University and Emerson College and have valued sports achievements ever since.

As fate would have it, my introduction to football broadcasting came in 1981, while an intern and an impressionable college student. I recall being the only female on the set of NBC's NFL '81 with Bryant Gumbel in New York City. Back then women I worked with were told they'd never be hired to anchor a sportscast or report on sports. Young "Pages" sent out tapes, hoping for a shot, but most news directors at that time wouldn't consider hiring a female to deliver a sportscast. I am delighted to have seen progress on that front through the years.

The universe works in amazing ways. Back in '81, while on the NBC set with Bryant Gumbel and Byron Day, Day reported from the field in "The 1981 Freezer Bowl" AFC Championship Game between Cincinnati and San Diego, the same game Gary Burley played in. Gumbel manned the anchor desk. Ironically, Day is also living in Alabama. As of this writing, he is anchoring at Fox 10 in Mobile, Alabama. Somehow, all three of us landed in Alabama. What are the odds? Burley asked me to collaborate on this special effort.

Speaking of Bryant Gumbel, my favorite behind-the-scenes memory from NFL '81 was watching the talented anchor watch multiple football games concurrently. Then while on camera, without using notes, or reading from a teleprompter, he summarized the highlights of each play descriptively, back-timing his words perfectly as the cameraman stood by the lens and counted down the seconds. Few broadcasters were as comfortable in front of the camera as he seemed to be.

Another favorite memory was watching producers carry Bryant Gumbel's wailing 3-year-old out of a cavernous broadcast studio moments before Gumbel went back on the air. You'd think he would be frazzled but rather appeared composed and engaged. I've always appreciated this uncanny ability to pull it all together and focus!

I learned the best performers have likable, authentic communication styles that draw the viewer in while they seem to remain cool under fire. I am humbled by the great teachers I have been surrounded by in my career, many of whom worked behind the scenes. Some of the more visible talents whose names you might recognize include Larry King, Leslie Stahl, Charles Osgood, Cokie Roberts, Steve Kroft, Bob Schieffer, Peter King, and countless others.

Health Challenges

I am convinced Gary Burley has 9 lives! He faces each challenge head-on with fearlessness and grace. Health challenges leave me humbled and thrilled to have a second lease on life. Gary and I both feel our lives were spared in part so that we could write this manuscript for you. If we encourage you to push through a rough patch and go on to achieve greater heights, then our efforts are worthwhile. Gary and I both realize how fortunate we have been to have survived unexpected and unforeseen physical challenges. These hindrances pale in comparison to what the five athletes faced in their lifetimes.

Young people often feel invulnerable. Yet age brings wisdom and that feeling of invulnerability erodes. In researching the 5 athletes highlighted in this book, we are inspired by how these remarkable men handled numerous challenges including injuries, health problems, discrimination, poverty, and countless impediments.

Life was proceeding nicely until 2018. While anchoring part-time for WCBS-AM, a NewsRadio station in New York City, I suddenly lost hearing in my right ear. I was later diagnosed with an acoustic neuroma (benign brain tumor) that required radiation treatments. Over the next year, I slowly lost function as I developed hydrocephalus (water on the brain). I developed headaches that felt like I was balancing a 30-pound bag on my head, had difficulty walking and fell, lost balance and coordination, developed bladder incontinence, nausea, vomiting, lethargy, memory loss, an inability to drive, lift, and most frighteningly, developed mild dementia. When discovered, the abundance of fluid in the brain required emergency surgery, and a brain shunt was installed to drain excess fluid. I recuperated for months with the help of physical therapy 3 times a week.

Despite radiation treatments that targeted the now large-sized brain tumor, it continued to grow, pressing on my brain stem. The enlarged tumor had become life-threatening. It caused confusion. Disfiguring facial spasms marred my appearance. In July of 2022, I faced my fears and underwent a second surgery, this time to evict the unwelcome growth.

While recovering from the surgeries and radiation, I worked to retrieve as many vocabulary words from my brain as possible. Writing this book helped! The three of us worked together as a team with Gary as our coach.

In the fall of 2022, Gary suffered a stroke and needed brain surgery.

Ralph and I continued our research. When Ralph was hospitalized, Gary and I pressed on. We feel the Creator slowed things down in our lives so that we could collaborate on this endeavor. We marvel that between us, we had survived 3 brain surgeries. We feel a greater force has brought the team together to demonstrate and inspire young people to face obstacles head-on.

Mottos

I want to leave you with some words of wisdom that inspired me. Live your dreams. I once read that *"If you can dream it, you can become it."* It's true! Because, *"Where there's a will, there's a way."*

Bless you and thank you for reading about some of these incredible individuals! May the lives of the men we write about encourage you and motivate you to achieve your dreams and carve out your own journey.

Bryant Gumbel (left), host of NFL '81 and
Donna Francavilla (right), when a Rutgers University college intern

Donna Francavilla
Owner of Frankly Speaking Communications LLC

Meet Dr. Valencia Belle

Sound Advice from Expert Dr. Valencia Belle

Contributor Dr. Valencia Belle is the Founder of two programs, S.C.H.O.O.L.S. for scholars and C.L.E.A.R.E.D for scholar-athletes.

S.C.H.O.O.L.S., or Success Can Happen Out Of Low Scores, affords high-quality, cost-effective standardized test prep to scholars and scholar-athletes, occasioning 5-10 point ACT and SAT 100 -200 point average composite score increases with as little as five weeks of test prep. These composite score gains have been shown statistically to eradicate inter-generational poverty for up to 3 generations occasioned by college-loan debt by enabling the attainment of presidential full-ride scholarships with refunds, especially for demographics stemming from marginalized communities.

C.L.E.A.R.E.D., a program specifically catered for scholar-athletes, focuses on obtaining NCAA D1 Clearance with matching GPAs and ACT/

SAT scores. A primary focus is the acquisition of intangible and marketable soft skills necessary to deal with "the mess, the press, and the stress" of instilling accountability for personal ownership by the scholar-athlete of his or her personal brand management through self-identification and critical thinking skills training for implementation in the classroom, the media and beyond - both on and off the field, track or court.

Dr. Belle is one of six inaugural recipients worldwide of the prestigious 2021 Wharton Knowledge For Impact Awards from the University of Pennsylvania's Wharton School of Business, as well as a 2019 Scholarship Recipient from Harvard University's Institute of Urban School Leaders.

She has authored "The Seven Women Every Woman Should Know", "The Belle Method of Academic Currency", and contributed toward "Glory: The Struggle For Yards." Her test prep expertise with S.C.H.O.O.L.S. has been featured nationally and internationally, having served most recently as a featured speaker for the 2021 ACAN Conference for Alabama Possible.

Receiving her Doctorate in Education, with a concentration in Organizational Change and Leadership, from the University of Southern California in 2023, Dr. Belle was named as a 2023 23 Women in Tech by Business Alabama Magazine, earned induction into the 2023 Murphy High School Hall of Fame, received the prestigious 2023 ASU+GSV G Cup Elite 200 Award for Ed-Tech, and won the 2022 Alabama Launchpad's Social Impact Seed Round Award Competition.

Dr. Belle's Advice:

With high-quality and cost-effective ACT PREP, the Belle Method of Academic Currency was demonstrated at Harvard, MIT, USC, and Wharton.

We begin standardized test prep as early as the Third Grade to prepare our students for qualification for such prestigious programs as the Duke TIP and National Merit Scholarship Programs.

For a minimal investment of time and money, that is, the cost of the actual ACT and the cost of the SCHOOLS ACT Prep Intensive, multiple parents and students have saved HUNDREDS of THOUSANDS of DOLLARS in college costs.

Editor's Note

The authors collectively hope you find inspiration between these pages. Each of the five players we selected to feature here has lived passionately and contributed in some significant way. We identified many little-known players who accomplished great things, but decided to focus this book on just 5 special men. We have only scratched the surface. It is our sincere hope that health, love, joy and all the good things in life come your way.

Sincerely, The Authors

Printed in the United States
by Baker & Taylor Publisher Services